16/2
75p

EAST SUSSEX INNS

EAST SUSSEX INNS

Brigid Chapman

With Illustrations by the author

COUNTRYSIDE BOOKS
NEWBURY, BERKSHIRE

ISBN 1 85306 022 4

Cover illustration by John Baker

Produced through MRM Associates, Reading
Typeset by J&L Composition Ltd, Filey, North Yorkshire
Printed in England by J.W. Arrowsmith Ltd., Bristol

To Nigel, with love

Acknowledgements

Many people have helped most kindly and patiently with the research for this book. Mrs Elizabeth Doff gave me the benefit of her extensive knowledge of the history of the Ouse Valley and Rushlake Green areas as did members of Warbleton and a number of other local history societies in East Sussex.

Miles Jenner of Harvey's Brewery in Lewes and John Hamblyn, surveyor of Charringtons at Newhaven provided vital information about their breweries' houses and Mr Christopher Wells supplied the story behind the white horse on the roof of the White Horse at Bodle Street Green.

Mrs Pat Berry, accosted in the Sussex Archeological Society's library in Lewes, forsook her own research to supply details of the pubs of Seaford which had been collected by the Seaford Museum of Local History.

Mrs Anne Hilton, deputy editor of the Sussex Express, contributed interesting references to the licensed houses in the Forest Row area and other colleagues on that newspaper helped me a lot with stories about the pubs in their areas.

The staff at the East Sussex County Library in Lewes were consistently helpful and encouraging and the licensees, who patiently answered my questions about the history of their houses, did everything they could to help. Thank you all so much.

INTRODUCTION

THERE IS a lot more to the pubs of East Sussex than the welcome they provide, the drinks they sell, the food they serve and the games that are played in them. The 'locals' sandwiched between the newsagents and the launderette in the large coastal towns, the 1930s style roadhouses on the trunk roads, the seaside taverns, the cosy country inns, the three star hotels – all have a past. Things happened in them. Exciting things, funny things, mysterious things, frightening things. . . .

The first pubs in Sussex catered principally for the Roman army of occupation. Wine was imported from the Mediterranean area to slake the thirst of the legions as they marched from Anderida to Noviomagus and back but the troops soon developed a taste for the local brew, much to the disgust of Pliny the Elder who described ale as a 'drink for barbarians'.

In AD 410 the legions were called back to Rome and the native Britons faced another invader – the Angles, Saxons and Jutes from North Germany and the Baltic. These Anglo-Saxons were great ones for their ale – so great, in fact, that some controls over their drinking had to be introduced. Their King Edgar, who reigned from AD 957–975 restricted the number of ale houses (from the Old English word aleu-hus) to one per village. For the average Anglo-Saxon drinking was a communal activity. So communal, in fact, that large wooden tankards would be passed from hand to hand and the ale in them was measured by wooden pegs placed at half pint intervals. Hence the expressions 'have a peg' and 'take him down a peg'.

The coming of Christianity, with its attendant churches, shrines and monasteries, increased the demand for places of rest and refreshment. The churches and abbeys had to be built and for this purpose large numbers of workmen would be concentrated at specific sites. They needed to be housed, fed and watered which accounts for the fact that close to every early church in the county is an early inn – or the remains of one. The Star at Old Heathfield was built to accommodate the stonemasons working on the church that preceded the present All Saints and became an alehouse in 1388, run by a stonemason called Wasseline Maydlow.

As religion became more organized it involved even more people. Pilgrims began to crisscross the country from shrine to shrine, venerating the relics on display and always hoping for a miracle. The monks saw these pilgrims as a source of revenue and did everything to encourage their interest. They built hospices for them and provided every comfort, for which their guests were expected to pay according to their means. A nobleman putting up, say, at the Star at Alfriston, would get the finest wine from France, the most spacious bedchamber, venison from the Abbot of Battle's woods and carp from his fishponds. The less wealthy and well connected would get beer brewed by the brothers, plenty of plain food and a dry bed for the night.

The church was also not slow to cash in on the fund raising potential of a good brew. Church ales, the precursors of the present day coffee mornings and garden fêtes, were introduced to raise money for the parish – perhaps for repairs to the church or to send young Ranúlph off to the Crusades. The parishioners would provide the barley and the church-wardens would brew strong ale from it which the congregation quaffed on the premises – inside in winter, in the churchyard on warm days. This quaffing could be excessive and incurred the disapproval of St Dunstan. When he was Archbishop of Canterbury he issued a number of edicts about unseemly behaviour at church ales and against intemperance by the clergy.

These edicts had little effect. Soon there were all sorts of ales – bride ales, wedding ales, midsummer ales – for what the church had started the laity continued. Bottle parties had begun.

It was the Puritans who put a stop to them. And to gambling, playing at cards, dice, quoits, horse racing, even dancing round the maypole. They imposed heavy taxes on ale and beer, made attendance at Divine Service compulsory, and had heavy penalties for anyone caught in an alehouse at church time.

This dismal state of affairs lasted for 11 years and England never totally recovered from it. Once a tax has been imposed it is rarely lifted and Charles II's return to the throne was a little help to brewers and innkeepers. In 1689 the tax was raised from 2s a barrel to 3s 3d and with the outbreak of the war with France it went up to 6s 6d a barrel.

About this time an Act was passed permitting Englishmen to distil spirits from home grown corn. It was done with the best of intentions – to curtail imports of brandy from France and to increase the demand for home grown grain – but its effects on the health of the nation were disastrous.

The spirit that everyone started to distil was genever or gin – a colourless liquor brought over from the Low Countries by William of Orange.

The horrors of the cheap gin era were not exaggerated by Hogarth in his series of engravings on the debauching effects of the drink. In the London area, between 1740 and 1742 there were twice as many burials as baptisms. In one year alone 6 million gallons of distilled spirits were consumed by 6 million people, among them little children. Pubs would advertise: 'Drunk for a penny, dead drunk for twopence, and the straw is free'!

It slowly dawned on both Church and State that something would have to be done to stop people drinking themselves to death. The licensing laws were tightened up considerably, heavy taxes were imposed on spirits, and the temperance movement was started. These measures helped but it was really the increasing availability of such non-alcoholic beverages as tea, coffee and chocolate that stopped Britain's long binge. Soon the cup that cheers but does not inebriate was at everyone's lips and philanthropist Jonas Hanway – he who made the umbrella fashionable – was writing: 'The people themselves seem at length to have discovered that health and pleasure, food and raiment, are better than sickness and pain, want and wretchedness'.

The early 18th century merchant adventurers ranged far

and wide to collect silks and spices, teas and coffee beans, to meet home demand and Parliament rewarded their efforts by slapping huge import taxes on almost everything. These taxes encouraged smuggling – in fact they caused it – and soon communities everywhere had their own gangs of free-traders to supply the parson with his brandy and the clerk with his tobacco. Smuggling brought business to the innkeepers of East Sussex which was nicely sited for the importation of contraband with plenty of safe anchorages along its coastline and good overland routes to London. Later, as the gangs got greedy, it also brought a reign of terror to some towns and villages. The heaviest mob of the lot was the Hawkhurst Gang, members of which would sit in the Mermaid Inn at Rye, blatantly displaying the goods they had smuggled – and the cutlasses they carried in case the Revenue men felt like a fight.

There was a pitched battle in Bexhill between 45 Excise officers and 16 smugglers armed with stout ash poles. It resulted in the death of three Revenue men, and the capture of eight smugglers; and there was another conflict outside the Star at Normans Bay in which the new coastguards were the victors and three smugglers were killed.

The smugglers brought some business to some inns but it was the coming of the coaches which brought a spell of real prosperity. As the roads were improved so were the vehicles that travelled on them and soon an efficient transport network had been built up with the inns acting as staging posts with a supply of fresh horses and accommodation for coachmen, grooms and, of course, the travelling public.

Old timber-fronted taverns were refaced with stone and coachhouses and stabling built behind them. The usual approach to this inner courtyard would be through an archway, which could be a bit dangerous for the outside passenger. The story of one who forgot to duck is told by Mr Jingle in the *Pickwick Papers*: 'Other day – five children mother – tall lady, eating sandwiches – forgot the arch – crash-knock – children look round – mother's head off – sandwich in her hand – no mouth to put it in – head of family off – shocking! shocking!'

It was not only archways which were a hazard for coach

passengers. The horses could bolt, traces could break, wheels come off, and deep potholes cause shafts to splinter. When the Brighton to Eastbourne coach left the White Horse, Rottingdean, one night after changing horses it disappeared completely. A day later it was found at the foot of the cliffs at Saltdean, passengers, horses and coachman all dead. It had been blown over by the strength of the wind.

Quite suddenly the constant bustle in the coaching inns was stilled. The arrival of the railway killed their business almost overnight and many of them closed their doors for good. Some were turned into private houses, others crumbled into dereliction, some survived by selling out to the local brewery and agreeing to serve only its beers, wines and spirits.

New names began to appear on inn signs in the towns and villages served by the new railway. There was a rash of Railway Taverns, Station Hotels, even an occasional Locomotive or Rocket.

These new railway pubs were built to a pattern with the bars divided into compartments, usually by mahogany and glass partitions, to separate first, second and third class customers, as the trains did. As well as saloon bars, public bars, lounge bars, ladies' bars, smoking rooms, vaults, tap rooms, private bars and snugs there were sometimes Shades.

This word for a bar or bars at the side or rear of larger premises has spread throughout the world but it originated in Brighton. In 1816 Edmund Savage, the first licensee of the Royal Pavilion Hotel in Castle Square did a deal with the bank next door. He acquired some of the back rooms of the bank, which adjoined his property, and planned to convert them into a smoke room and gin shop and call it the Gin Palace. But Mrs Fitzherbert, whose house was immediately opposite, objected most strongly to the prospect of looking out onto premises bearing the words 'Gin Palace' on its sign. She made her objections known to Mr Savage, and he, well aware of her connections with the Prince Regent, made a quick compromise. He looked at the height of Mrs Fitzherbert's house and he looked at the bit of the bank he planned to turn into his new bar. 'As the sun cannot shine on my bar I will christen it Shades' he said.

Hardly had the licensed trade adjusted to the railways and was looking towards the motor car and the motor omnibus for a new kind of carriage trade when the war clouds gathered once again. This time not only were taxes on beer and spirits increased to pay for the costs of the conflict but the hours in which people could drink were restricted. It was Lloyd George's attempt to get the British people to concentrate wholly on the war effort. 'In my opinion there are three enemies – Germany, Austria and drink – and as far as I can see the greatest of these deadly foes is drink' he said. In 1915 he introduced the Defence of the Realm Act, the dreaded DORA, and for the first time pubs were not allowed to open when they wanted to. In areas where it was considered essential for the war effort they could not open before noon, or between 2.30pm and 6pm. Six years later these restrictions were confirmed by the Licensing Act and extended to nearly all licensed premises.

In the First, as in the Second World War, there were numbers of troops from all parts of the world stationed in Sussex. The presence of some Canadians in Lewes caused the British Army to do something totally unprecedented – it closed a pub. The White Swan in Malling Street, which started its licensed life as the King and Queen in the 17th century when it was owned by the church of St Thomas à Becket, was a favourite haunt of the Canadians. One night some British Tommies made a take-over bid for the premises and, at the end of the affray, a Canadian soldier was found stabbed to death on the doorstep. There were mutterings in the Canadians' ranks about revenge and the situation was tense. To prevent further trouble and possibly further bloodshed the innkeeper, Samuel Moon, was ordered to close for the duration. The White Swan never opened as an inn again. For years it was used as a furniture store and then by the Electricity Board, also as a storeroom. At the time of writing the timber-framed building is undergoing extensive renovation and there are antiques for sale in its coachhouses at the rear.

Sussex was very much in the front line in the Second World War. The first high explosives fell on Ticehurst on 22nd May

1940 and many pubs were burned, bombed or blasted out of existence. The Bell at Shortgate was a casualty, the Plough at Seaford was badly damaged. The ones that remained open often became headquarters for the local Home Guard or ARP, accommodated people in their cellars during air raids, provided bottles of black market booze to the troops from the back door and generally did their bit. Everything was under the counter in those days – except the customers who could not get enough to drink to put them there.

The past 40 or so years of comparative peace have seen more huge changes in the licensed trade. Most of the spit and sawdust pubs have gone, to be replaced by warmer, better furnished, more comfortable places. Instead of a pint by the porch and a packet of peanuts the customer has a choice of beers, wines, spirits and liqueurs. There are usually salads or hot snacks, proper lunches and evening meals, quite often a restaurant attached specialising in particular delicacies.

Not only are the inns of East Sussex catering for the whole family but they are caring for the wider community as well. The Milk and Ale Club members at the Grenadier in Hailsham have just bought their 21st guide dog for the blind, regulars at the Lewes Arms perform their own Christmas pantomime for charity, and rarely a week goes past without a report in the local papers about sponsored sports, piles of pennies, darts marathons and similar events for good causes.

The pubs of the past could be perilous places, as the following pages will show. Today patrons are not at risk from attacks by highwaymen, forcible conscription into the Armed Forces by the press gangs, or the likelihood of a fall down the unguarded cellar steps. All they have to worry about is getting a lift home from an abstemious friend – if they live too far away to walk and do not wish to be breathalysed.

The Merrie Harriers, Cowbeech

ALCISTON

ROSE COTTAGE: It all happens outside this one time cottage alehouse on Good Friday. The narrow village street leading to the Downs is packed with cars and people. They have all come to watch the skipping.

They used to skip at Brighton's fishmarket on Good Friday until the last war brought barbed wire onto the beaches. They skipped in the back streets of Hove, and at Scarborough, and at Hastings. The practice died out around the turn of the century but it was revived at Alciston after the Second World War when a party of skippers walked over the Downs from Newhaven with a long rope. By 1954 the practice had become so well established that the *Sussex County Magazine* reported that 13 members of one family had turned up for the skipping. Regrettably the family was not named, but there was a photograph.

Quite why they skip on Good Friday has never been satisfactorily explained. It appears to be a maritime custom, perhaps associated with the drying out of ropes and nets. However, folklorists favour a fertility dance explanation. They say that early man used to encourage the growth of crops by stamping on the ground in springtime. There is even a Cretan hymn advising young men and women to 'leap for full jars, fields of fleecy flocks and hives to bring increase'.

Whatever the reason, skipping outside the Rose Cottage on Good Friday has become a Sussex tradition and now the ceremony is faithfully performed by members of the Knots in May Folk Dance Group.

ALFRISTON

MARKET CROSS INN: There are always good tales to tell about inns associated with smugglers. The Market Cross with its 21 rooms, six staircases, 48 doors, numerous corridors and secret hiding places was so closely associated with the Alfriston gang that it became more generally known as the Smugglers.

It was here, so the stories go, that the gang led by Stanton Collins, had its headquarters and concealed the contraband brought up from the Cuckmere Haven. And it was here that a pig was used to dupe the Revenue men. There are two versions of the pig tale. One has it that a smuggler who was being hunted was concealed beneath the bed of a woman about to go into labour. His friends pushed a pig from a nearby sty under the bed with him and when he heard his pursuers approach he pinched the animal to make it squeal. Thinking that they had heard the cry of a new born babe the officers did not enter the bedroom.

In the second version the smugglers had stolen a pig – trade in contraband being quiet at the time. When the law officers came searching for it they put a sack around its body and a bonnet on its head and placed it between the sheets beside Mrs Stanton Collins who was lying in bed ill. The law officers looked into the room but left quietly without disturbing mother and 'child'.

Deeds in the East Sussex Records Office show that in 1815, the year of the Battle of Waterloo, James Collins, a butcher of Chiddingly, bought Market Cross House in the High Street of Alfriston. He passed it on to his son, Stanton, in 1823, who four years later mortgaged part of the property – referred to as 'a warehouse, cottage, slaughterhouse and buildings recently erected and let to the parish overseers as an alms-house for paupers belonging to the parish'. In a deed of 1844 the warehouse had become a brewhouse. But Stanton Collins was never an innkeeper. The *Sussex Weekly Advertiser* reports that at the Lewes Winter Assizes of 1831 he was sentenced to seven years transportation for 'stealing 12 baskets of barley and three sacks'.

STAR INN: For many years historians have been arguing about the origins of this 15th century inn and what its medieval woodcarvings represent. The generally accepted view is that it started life as a hospice set up by the monks at Battle Abbey for the care and comfort of pilgrims on their way from Canterbury to the shrine of St Richard at Chichester. The carvings are a mishmash of the sacred and the secular with a bit of heraldry thrown in. There are monkeys and mitred bishops, snakes, a dragon being slain by St Michael (or is it St George?) gargoyles and the sacred symbol IHS incised in Gothic letters in a beam.

Of later date is the red painted lion-like wooden figure at the southern corner of the inn. According to yet another local smugglers' tale it was the figurehead of a ship wrecked off Cuckmere Haven and cleared of its cargo in two nights by Stanton Collins and his gang. He is said to have taken a liking to the lion and put it outside Market Cross House when he lived there. There is no record of how or when or why it was moved to the Star.

Another theory is that the figurehead came from a Dutch ship wrecked in the Channel after the Battle of Southwold in 1672. This conflict between the navies of the Netherlands and England reached no definite conclusion because the contestants were scattered by a severe storm. One Dutchman was washed up on the Suffolk coast and its lion figurehead ended up outs de the Red Lion in Martlesham. Photographs of both figureheads are in the March 1934 issue of the *Sussex County Magazine* and the resemblance is striking.

GEORGE INN: Repeated alterations and a fire behind the public bar in 1942 have brought many changes to this 15th century inn which in the coaching era was the village's

principal resting place for travellers. Half the Horsham stone roof has gone and the arched entrance to the stables and coach-houses has been incorporated into the hotel. At one time these stables housed the horses and the carriages of its turn-of-the-century landlord, Joseph Dumbrell, the local fly proprietor.

Later they were used by a builder to store materials and then by a garage business. In the late 1930s the tile-hung front was stripped from the oak-framed building to expose its beamed façade and Victorian sash windows were replaced by others more in keeping with the age of the inn. During this restoration some 16 layers of wallpaper were removed from a room on the first floor and wall paintings dating from the late 16th century were revealed. They are of a stylised floral pattern and framed by the oak panels of the walls.

It was from the George Inn on 4th December 1775 that Mr Stephen Wood set out to walk, for a considerable wager, the 18 miles to Lewes and back in five hours. 'Notwithstanding that he was 54 years of age and a very heavy rain fell the whole time he did the walk in four hours, 20 minutes. There were many heavy bets depending and the knowing ones were deeply taken in' reports the *Sussex Weekly Advertiser*.

ARLINGTON

YEW TREE INN: For nearly 100 years tenants of this inn paid their rent to the parish church – or rather to its churchwardens and overseers. For in 1766 William Harmer and his wife, Ann, granted the church a 999 year lease on the premises.

The lease was assigned in 1837 to the Rev Thomas Scutt of Clapham House, Litlington, whose executors sold it to Herbert Lynn of Hailsham Brewery. This brewery, with its tied houses, the Yew Tree and the Welcome Stranger at Herstmonceux, was sold by auction in 1912. By 1928 the Yew Tree was a free house. It had been bought by a former tenant, Albert Edward Kelly, but 10 years later it was acquired by the Star Brewery of Eastbourne, which was taken over in 1965 by Courage. The Yew Tree is now a Harvey's house.

OLD OAK INN: This house was built in 1733 for £231 11s 6d as the village poorhouse and it did not become an inn until after the passing of the Poor Law Amendment Act in 1834. This Act changed the system which had existed since 1601 which required parishes to look after their own poor. In rural areas this often caused terrible hardship. The poor were kept in appalling conditions because workers on starvation wages had little to spare for those even less well off than themselves.

But in 1733 the parish of Arlington had somehow acquired sufficient funds to do its duty by its poor. The churchwardens and overseers decided 'with all due convenient expedition' to build a house on a piece of land at Cane Heath belonging to the parish. It was to be of brick and to have two single chimneys and two double with three hearths to each chimney.

The cost of the bricks, tiles, timber, doors, windows, glazing and plastering is all listed in the churchwardens' and over-

seers' account book covering the years 1723–68 which is now in the East Sussex Records Office. It was discovered in the wall of an old cottage being demolished at Locks Farm, Halland in 1957. After 1834 parishes were divided into groups each of which was served by a central warehouse, called the Union. When Arlington's poor were moved to Hailsham the old poorhouse was turned into an alehouse which opened on Sundays only. On other days of the week the workers it was intended to serve were too busy working in the woods to break off for a drink of the alewife's home brew. The inn, now with a full on licence, keeps up its arboreal connections. Customers can buy Christmas trees as well as drinks there at Christmas time.

BATTLE

GEORGE HOTEL: Francis Grose, the Richmond Herald and Fellow of the Society of Arts went on a sketching tour of Sussex in 1777. He was accompanied by the Rev William Hayley, vicar of Brightling and a kinsman of Sir William Burrell. After visiting Battle Abbey they dropped into the George for dinner but, unlike the other 18th century Sussex tourist, John Byng, Grose makes no mention in his diary of what he had to eat or how well, or badly, he was served.

An addition of an assembly room shortly after Grose's visit made this coaching inn a social centre for the neighbourhood. Balls were held in it for the officers of the regiments stationed in the area during the Napoleonic wars and the first Battle Flower Show was held here in 1834. Coaches ran daily the 8 miles to and from the Swan in Hastings when Joseph Couchman was the landlord. Eight years later Henry Ducquer advertised that a pair horse brake would leave the hotel every Tuesday for Normanhurst Court, the house built by railway contractor Thomas Brassey when he retired to Sussex in 1865 at the age of 60. Lord Brassey, who also built 40 miles of railway in the Crimea, died before Normanhurst Court was completed and his son, who became MP for Hastings succeeded to its 3,000 acres. He was passionate about the sea and in 1876, with his wife, circumnavigated the globe.

BEXHILL

BELL INN: In Diplock's Guide of 1816, when this was a busy posting house, it was described as 'a good and convenient inn with every accommodation calculated for the reception of strangers who, in summer, are frequently induced to visit this rural spot'. There was a small theatre attached to the premises which was also used as an assembly room. It was here, in June 1819, that a number of elderly men were entertained to dinner to celebrate King George III's 80th birthday. In the chair for the occasion was a sprightly 84 year old and the youngest of the 46 people present was 75 and there were several of 87. Only three of the veteran partygoers died under the age of 80 and several of them reached the age of 92.

It was in this assembly room in 1884 that local government came to Bexhill, the need for it sparked off by a typhoid epidemic caused by bad drains. Some authority was needed to sort out these drains. The newly constituted Local Board of Bexhill met regularly at the Bell, moving later to the Institute in Station Road and then to the Town Hall when it was opened in 1895.

But it was not all celebrations and civic affairs in 19th century Bexhill. The town had a seamier side – a thriving smuggling industry. There was a running fight outside the Bell in January 1828 between some 45 Revenue men and 16 smugglers armed with stout ash poles. It ended with the death of three Revenue men, one smuggler found hacked to bits, and another crippled for life. Eight smugglers were captured after this bloody battle and transported to New South Wales.

More violence came the Bell's way in the last war. One of the 485 flying bombs that passed over the town in one period of 24 hours fell on Belle Hill and did a lot of damage to the premises.

DEVONSHIRE: South London builder and contractor John Webb came to Bexhill to build the sea wall between Galley Hill and Sea Lane for £34,000 and a gift of some land south of the railway line.

When he had finished his wall, laid out a large part of the Egerton Park estate, and built quite a lot of the present town centre, he built an hotel on the land he had been given. He became the first proprietor of the Devonshire Hotel which quickly became the social centre of the new town which was springing up south of the railway.

In 1892 he sold it to another member of the Bexhill establishment, Mr R C Sewell, who ran it for the next 30 years. Mr Sewell was an enthusiastic member of the local council and when he was mayor the borough bought the water and gas undertakings which had been in private hands since the 1880s. Also acquired were the powers to build the De La Warr Pavilion. For his contribution to civic life in the borough Mr Sewell received the Freedom of Bexhill in 1952 – its golden jubilee year.

The Devonshire did not survive as an hotel for long after that. Its ballroom, said to have the best dance floor in the district, was closed and today there is just a long busy bar.

BLACKBOYS

BLACKBOYS INN: A woman died tragically in childbirth while her parents continued to serve their customers in the bar parlour. The ghost of poor Anne Starr is now said to haunt this inn which was built as a farmhouse in 1389 and converted to an alehouse when iron foundries were opened in the area.

Anne, the daughter of Mr and Mrs Thomas Starr, was born in 1765. She was, at 38, a plain unmarried spinster of the parish but romance came into her life when her cousin, William, came to work for her parents. He seduced her in the four-poster bed in the room above the bar, having promised to marry her. But as soon as he found out that she was pregnant he left to find work elsewhere and never did return. Anne's baby was stillborn and she suffered agonies at its birth but her parents ignored her cries and she died alone and unattended. She is buried in Framfield churchyard, but it is said that she can be heard pacing about the bedroom above the bar – and on some nights her cries can be heard.

Blackboys and its inn are, in some accounts, said to be called after the young men covered with charcoal who worked in the iron foundries where the railings for St Paul's church were cast in the 17th century. But it is more likely that the name came from a former Lord of the Manor, Sir Philip Blakeboys.

British actor and star of many film comedies, Ronald Shiner, owned the inn in the 1950s until his death at Eastbourne in 1966. It was the RAF comedy *Worms Eye View*, both the play and the film, that made him a household name and another of his long-running plays was *Seagulls over Sorrento*.

There are stocks on the green outside the pub and inside is a fine stag's head for the game of Ring the Bull. The pub record was set up in 1952/3 by Bill Harris who ringed the stag with 58 consecutive throws.

BODLE STREET GREEN

WHITE HORSE:This inn was built in 1850 by Richard Oxley, son of Mrs Philadelphia Oxley, some 50 yards away from the original White Horse which, with the exception of its cellars, was demolished in 1886. It was later rebuilt as a private house, now called the Birches.

Edward Peter Pankhurst was the innkeeper in the 1880s and brewed his own beer and cider which was much to the liking of the farmworkers of the district after days of heavy manual labour in the fields. But in spite of their thirst the inn was not busy enough to give Mr Pankhurst a living so he opened up a wheelwright's shop as well. In the end that was not enough and he went bankrupt. But when the bailiffs called, Edward Pankhurst was a match for them. He offered them so much hospitality that they collapsed dead drunk and he was able to move all the tools of his trade to a place of safety before they woke up.

A later licensee was Mr Fred Brett who brought the first motor car to the village. It was a 1922 Model T Ford. Fred Brett had lost an arm in France in the First World War and he kept as a paperweight the nose cone of the bomb that blew it off. He managed to drive quite happily with one arm and to pull pints and often had a battle of words with the village policeman for serving drinks to under age children around Christmas time.

A large white horse is painted on the tiled roof of the inn. Before the war it was a portrait of the racehorse owned by a director of the Star Brewery, then owners of the inn, and it faced to the right. It had to be painted out in the Second World War in case it was used as a target by German bombers. When it was replaced in peacetime it was painted facing to the left.

In the 1960s business was brisk at the White Horse but then trade fell off and in 1972 it closed down for a year. It was then bought as a free house by architect and builder Michael Ramsden who installed a new porch, interior oak beams, and had the present white horse painted on the roof.

BOREHAM STREET

BULL'S HEAD: In 1788 John Byng, a Lieutenant Colonel in the Life Guards and later to become the fifth Earl of Tortington, toured the South of England by horse, coach and on foot, and kept a record of his travels. His was the first good food guide or good inn guide because he comments at some length on the comfort and the menus provided at the hostelries he visited.

The Bull's Head gets three stars: 'I walked my horse to Boreham' he says. 'Here was a most tempting public house and it was now the right hour of appetite so I ordered cold beef to be laid forth in a clean bow-windowed room. Our stay here was long and comfortable – all neatness within, all beauty without.'

BREDE

RED LION: Something happened in this village inn which helped to change the course of history. On tithe audit day in 1830 the rector, the Rev H S Hele, son-in-law of the Bishop of Norwich met the local farmers in the bar parlour to talk about a reduction in tithes. Outside was an angry mob of farm labourers, their wives and children, fiercely demanding a living wage. This the farmers could not afford to pay them unless the tithe was reduced from £715 to £400. The rector, knowing the parish needed all the cash it could get to meet its obligations under the Poor Law Act of 1601 refused to reduce the tithe under intimidation.

This refusal, coupled with the cruel behaviour of the workhouse governor Thomas Abell, started a revolt that spread like wildfire throughout the country.

On the evening of 5th November, again in the Red Lion, the labourers' leaders and the farmers met together and passed two resolutions: firstly that every able bodied labourer with a wife and children should be paid 2s 3d a day until 1st March and from then to 1st October, 2s 6d a day; and secondly the overseer Mr Thomas Abell, should be taken out of the parish.

Word was sent to Abell that the mob was after him and he was advised to come out peacably. In answer he threatened to shoot the first man who meddled with him and appeared at his bedroom window with a shotgun. Two farmers, William Coleman and John Bourne, called to him to put the gun down and come out. He did so, although later he claimed that they had attacked him with bludgeons to get him to surrender.

Abell had incurred the hostility of the people of Brede by trying to stop the allowances for children of the families in his care at the poorhouse. This hostility turned to hatred when he harnessed men and women from the workhouse to a heavy cart and made them drag stone from the wharf up the steep hill to the village for road mending.

Abell was given a taste of his own medicine. He was put into the stone cart and dragged out of the parish, accompanied by a crowd of 500 cheering and jeering villagers, and dumped by the roadside near Robertsbridge.

When he got back to the workhouse the following day he was given three months notice by the parish overseers. But he had apparently learned his lesson for a month later the notice was withdrawn and when Abell eventually retired there were some fulsome tributes to his diligence.

As a result of the Brede Rising and other protests the Poor Law Amendment Act of 1834 was introduced and individual parishes were relieved of the responsibility of caring for their poor.

The 400 year old Red Lion also has a smuggling history. It was the headquarters of the Brede gang and the scene of several fierce fights between smugglers and the revenue men.

The leaders were the Whitemans and the Millers from nearby Udimore but their free-trading days were ended at the Horsham Spring Assize of 1828. Spencer Whiteman, two Millers and five others were indicted for assembling armed for the purposes of smuggling. They were sent for trial at the Old Bailey and were sentenced to death but this was commuted to transportation for life.

Another customer of the Red Lion to fall foul of authority was Thomas Netter. One day, in the year 1530, he was quietly supping his ale and reading his psalter when the rector, Sir Rauf Robynson, came in for a drink. He noticed that Netter was reading an English translation of the Latin psalter – then a most heinous offence. Netter was accused of heresy, had his psalter confiscated, and spent the next four days in the stocks.

BRIGHTLING

FULLER'S ARMS: Anything odd in this area is laid at the door of Mad Jack Fuller, the local squire of Brightling Park, builder of a number of follies and a troublesome Member of Parliament between 1801 and 1812.

So he is blamed for the village inn being outside the parish. There are two versions of the tale. In one it is said that he did a deal with the vicar and had the pub moved from directly opposite the church to its present site at Oxley Green in return for the vicar's agreement to him being buried in a pyramid tomb in the churchyard. In the other version it is said that the innkeeper offended Mad Jack in some way so he ordered his removal – inn and all.

The second version is most probably the correct one. The inn was opened at Oxley Green in 1834, the year Squire Fuller died. The pyramid shaped tomb in the churchyard was built years before. It was designed by architect Sir Robert Smirke and another local tale has it that Mad Jack sits inside it with a bottle of claret at his hand and surrounded by broken glass which he believed would cut the Devil's hooves should he drop in for a drink.

In 1775, when Mad Jack was just a teenager, the rector of Brightling was the Rev William Hayley. In a letter he wrote to his kinsman, Sir William Burrell, he says that the church is dedicated to St Thomas à Becket and that the wake or feast of its dedication is kept on the Monday after 7th July when the landlady of the inn, then called the Green Man, 'baked light cakes in the forenoon and puddings in the evening for sale.'

BRIGHTON

Regency, raffish queen of the watering places with a collapsing pier to the west and a new marina to the east – that was Brighton to most people until October 1984 when an IRA bomb went off and tore the heart out of the Grand Hotel and the Conservative Party conference. The Grand's gashes have been repaired and, in the pubs on and off the sea front, it is again business as usual.

OLD SHIP HOTEL: Oldest of Brighton's old inns and now offering three star comfort and with plush bars for drinking customers. Its history has been well recorded and it even has a book to itself – *The Old Ship* by Raymond Flower.

When Brighthelmstone was a small fishing village the Old Ship was a tiny tavern. It gained hotel status around 1750 when it was owned by William Hicks. His son, John, mortgaged the place to the hilt in 1794 to build assembly rooms to rival those of nearby, and now demolished, Castle Inn. A court martial was held in the new assembly rooms in 1795 at which

31

13 members of the Oxford Militia were charged with mutiny at East Blatchington. The trial lasted nine days and three of the mutineers were sentenced to be shot, two to be transported to Botany Bay, and six to be flogged. The remaining four were set free.

A concert of his own compositions was given by world famous violinist Niccolo Paganini in the assembly rooms on 9th December 1831. Other famous guests include Sir Henry Irving who used to walk each evening from the inn to the Theatre Royal to play his Hamlet; William Thackeray; and Charles Dickens.

The Tettersell bar in the Old Ship is named in memory of Brighthelmstone businessman Nicholas Tettersell who agreed to take the fleeing King Charles II across to France after the Battle of Worcester in 1651. Tettersell was the owner of the coaling brig *Surprise* and he accepted the charter for a fee of £60. After the Restoration he basked in royal approval and bought the Old Ship in 1670 and went on to become High Constable of Brighton.

HENEKEY'S NEW SHIP: In the 1930s this inn, across the road from the Old Ship, was given its present medieval mansion façade. It was the first coach office in Brighton and coaches started from its courtyard as early as 1741.

In the past it had guests who tended to disappear. First to go was the Rev James Gwynn, principal of Brasenose College, Oxford. He arrived at the New Ship on 14th August 1770 with his servant and ordered dinner. While it was being prepared he went for a walk and was never seen alive again. Some days later a little girl found a body in a barley field to the west of the town. It was Mr Gwynn. He was lying on his face, his whip at his side, and he was still wearing his gloves, boots and spurs. There were no marks of violence on the body and in his wallet there were three £100 banknotes.

Next guest to leave abruptly was the Chevalier Maupeau. On 10th September 1789 he took rooms at the inn and the following day his dead body was found under the hedge of a field, again on the west side of the town. The inquest verdict was that he had shot himself as a result of family troubles. He was said to have twice tried to drown himself on the sea passage from France. He left behind in his rooms a large amount of gold and silver, letters of credit on a number of London banks, two gold watches and three miniatures of a lovely lady, framed in gold.

A year later 37 elderly nuns were brought to the New Ship by the captain of the packet *Prince of Wales*, for which the inn was the booking agency. They had only £30 in cash between them and required almost all the available accommodation as they refused to sleep two to a bed. They were helped on their way by the Prince of Wales who, accompanied by Mrs Fitzherbert, his morganatic wife, visited them at the New Ship and agreed to launch a subscription fund for them. A total of £100 was raised and the nuns were able to continue their journey to Brussels.

There always seemed to be money around in some way at the New Ship. In October 1805 the licensee, Mr Baulcomb, had the 16th share in the winning ticket in the first lottery ever drawn in England. The prize was £20,000.

SEA HOUSE: This was originally called the Ship in Distress. In 1800 the innkeeper was James Leach and although all the windows of the main room faced the sea the entrance was from the east, at right angles to the shore. Over this front, or rather side door, was a picture of a foundering ship with the words:

> By danger we're encompassed round
> Pray lend a hand, our ship's aground.

In those days the sea front road ended at the inn and there was a causeway of planks, only passable in fair weather, from it to the eastern corner of West Street. In 1821 work started on making a carriage drive parallel to the sea and George IV contributed 200 guineas to the project, and performed the opening ceremony a year later.

In 1825/26 the Ship in Distress was rebuilt by John Galland

and its name was changed. The magistrates and the town's commissioners met there for a number of years and Brewster Sessions were held on the premises. The Brighton Tradesmen's Glee Club ended, however, on a sour note. Their last and most successful meeting was held at the Sea House and the club closed down because the innkeeper raised the hire charges.

In September 1830 a very important resident moved in. It was the Viscountess Bronte, widow of Admiral Lord Nelson, and during her stay she was visited by King William IV. They met in the coffee room and conversed together for three quarters of an hour.

THE CRICKETERS: This is one of the town's oldest inns and was originally called the Last and Fishcart – a 'last' being a measure of 10,000 fish. Above the front door was inscribed the verse:

> Long time I've looked for good beer
> And at 'The Last' have found it here.

The flint walled, bow windowed inn's name was changed in 1790 when it was taken over by a keen cricketer, Mr Jutten. He played in a great match on the Level in that year between Brighton and Wadhurst. The Prince of Wales was among the spectators but Brighton lost by three wickets. In the return match a week later Brighton were the victors by five wickets.

Jutten never made much of a showing in the big matches. In a four day game between Brighton and Mary-le-Bone (later the MCC) he only scored 2 runs before being run out.

Still in the saloon bar is an engraved glass lunette showing the pitch with the old-time cricketers at play.

LORD NELSON: In 1800, when the innkeeper was Richard Hobden, this was the Bell Inn and on its sign was an inverted bell with the couplet:

Good liquor here is to be found
The Bell's for luck turned upside down.

The name was changed to the Lord Nelson in 1890. About that time an inquest was held on the premises before coroner Mr G Gwynne, into the death of James Smith, a prizefighter who died from injuries received in a bout on the Race Hill for a purse of a sovereign. His opponent was Daniel Watts and the punch up was watched by a crowd of 3 to 4 thousand people. The jury returned a verdict of manslaughter against Watts and he was committed to Horsham jail to await his trial. A few days later he also died, of injuries he had received in the contest.

KING AND QUEEN: King George III and Queen Caroline were the monarchs first depicted on this inn's sign. It was built as a farmhouse in 1723 and licensed in 1779. It was here, in 1817, that a meeting was held to lay out the Valley Gardens and the Prince Regent contributed to the project which has survived to this day in the chain of gardens stretching from the Old Steine to St Peter's church.

Before the gardens were developed the level ground in front of the inn was the scene of a variety of sports and pastimes. In 1807 John Gully and John Cribb, both bare first boxing champions of England, sparred before a large crowd which included the Prince of Wales. For Cribb it was very much a home date as he was born within a stone' throw of the King and Queen.

Some four years later a conman was caught at the inn. John Fuller managed to persuade some of his fellow guests to each pay £2 for some fake banknotes and he was dragged to the pillory in North Street. This was the first time the pillory had been used as a punishment in Brighton and a crowd of 5,000 watched while Fuller stood with his head and hands in a block on a platform 10 to 12 feet above the ground. He stood there, facing the gibes and taunts of the spectators, from 12 noon to 1pm. There was an order against pelting the pilloried person with missiles, and offenders were threatened with imprisonment. All shops in the neighbourhood were closed while the sentence was being carried out.

Until the Corn Exchange was built in 1868 the ground floor of the inn housed the Brighton Corn Exchange and Horse Market. And as the barracks were immediately behind the premises one of the innkeepers, a former sergeant in the Hussars, had a hole made so liquor could be passed through to the soldiers.

In the 1930s the old inn was rebuilt in mock Tudor style and the King and Queen became Henry VIII and Anne Boleyn. The artist who designed the new interior was Ashley Tabb and during the demolition and rebuilding a case of coins was unearthed dating from the Hanoverian period. It included an Austrian coin and a forged George III shilling and a crude imitation of a Georgian halfpenny.

BEAR INN: Cock fighting and bear baiting were popular holiday attractions at this inn in the early part of the 19th century, according to contemporary newspaper accounts. The regulars were so devoted to their sport that they were prepared to travel to away fixtures. On Easter Monday in 1810 'to give an interesting variety to their sports' a bull was tied to a stake and baited at Hove 'which afforded some amusement at which the whole of the Bear assemblage was present'.

There was, however, a little trouble. 'The compact phalanx of gazers was broken through and put to rout by the rottenness of the rope which gave the bull its freedom', reports the *Sussex Advertiser*. 'The scene of confusion which ensued would be difficult to describe but happily no serious injuries marred the refined pleasures of the day.'

KINGS ARMS: In July 1816 this pub was the winning post in a race against time. Captain Wombwell of the 1st Life Guards, for a bet of 500 guineas, undertook to drive a tandem from Westminster Bridge to Brighton without changing horses. He started at 4am and, in spite of the rain which fell in torrents all the time, arrived at 8.45am having covered a distance of 52 miles in 4¾ hours.

BURWASH

ROSE AND CROWN: There were regular card parties here in the 18th century. An announcement in the *Sussex Weekly Advertiser* of 24th September 1787 gives these details: 'Burwash Card Assembly will commence on Wednesday, September 26 and continue on every Wednesday fortnight during the winter at the Rose and Crown Inn. W.Raynes (clerk).'

This rambling inn, which dates from 1570 is on the south

side of the former village square and near the cricket ground. The teams would bath after matches in one of the outhouses and the water would be heated in cauldrons on the inglenook fireplace. In the 19th century the Rose and Crown was a busy commercial hotel.

BEAR INN: Many 300 year old inns carry the scars of conflicts – but not many can show the actual bullet holes. There are four such holes in the blackened beam over the inglenook in the main bar and they got there one night in the 1940s when a Canadian soldier loosed off his revolver. Not so long ago another Canadian from the same unit called at the pub to see if the marks were still there.

Visitors from overseas more usually come to the Bear for the Kipling connection. It was here that the poet and story-teller stayed before he bought Bateman's and there is a memorial room off the main bar where the Kipling Society would meet. On the walls are photographs showing Kipling speaking at a recruiting rally and outside Buckingham Palace after a garden party.

CAMBER

ROYAL WILLIAM HOTEL: This inn got its name because its first licensee, William Morris had served aboard the *Royal William*, one of His Majesty's ships of the line, as ship's carpenter. In 1807 he came ashore to Camber, carved a model of the ship on which he had served as an inn sign, and opened for business. The sign was in place for many years but one day it disappeared – to turn up years later in a London auction house where it was bought by an American dealer and taken to the United States.

The barrels and casks in William Morris's inn used to rest on stands which stood along one wall and the wall between the saloon and public bar could be pulled back to make one large room for special occasions.

Some of the visitors were not always welcome. The press gangs were active in the area in the late 1860s and they frequented the inns which were then open all day and late into the night. If some likely lad could be engaged in conversation it was easy enough for a member of the press gang to drop a shilling into his pot of ale. If he drained his pot and found the coin he was said to have taken the King's shilling and would be carried away for military service. In those days most ale pots were made of pewter and the shilling was not visible to the drinker until it was too late. In later years pewter pots had glass bottoms so the coin could be easily spotted and the press gang avoided.

One Camber resident was nearly caught by the press gang. Edmund Duff Butchers went into Rye on business and called at the Queen's Head in Landgate for a drink before walking home. He spotted the press gang man drop a coin in his tankard so he took a few sips and put it on the bar counter. At this moment the press gang men pounced but as they tried to grab him he slipped away and ran down an alley, across the Salts and swam the river to get home to the Billy as the Royal William was then called.

The old inn was burned down in a disastrous fire and its site bought by Rye Golf Club. The new Royal William went up in 1936/37 at the corner of the Old Lydd Road and the Lydd Road but another fire destroyed the sea chest and a number of old charts belonging to the first innkeeper – old William Morris – which had survived the previous conflagration.

CATSFIELD

WHITE HART: Was this 19th century building the first inn on this site by the now vanished village green? If there was one before it, was it the Half Moon? So far it has not been possible to answer these questions and solve the mystery of the whereabouts of the alehouse that was the scene of an incident mentioned in successive editions of the *Sussex Weekly Advertiser*. On 11th January 1790, this report appears: 'A weaver from Crowhurst went out after debts owing him, collected £10, went to an alehouse at Catsfield Green and lost his money, all but 3d. He went home to bed but got up and hanged himself in an outhouse. Mr Justice Fuller, we hear, has very properly said that the unlawful proceedings which caused the poor weaver's melancholy catastrophe shall prevent the alehouse on the green from being licensed in the future.'

The following week, 18th January, we read: 'The master of the Half Moon public house on Catsfield Green in his justification said that the deceased did not lose so much as was stated, that he was always addicted to gambling and had before made attempts on his own life'.

Perhaps the innkeeper's plea in mitigation was not accepted and the alehouse lost its licence? Or did the weaver really go to the Half Moon at nearby Battle, now the Abbey Hotel, and the paper got the address wrong?

The present pub is a great centre for games, but of the sporting rather than the gambling kind.

CHAILEY

FIVE BELLS: With the coming of the turnpike road in 1752 this old alehouse was extended and became a busy coaching inn. It took its name from the five bells in the tower of the nearby church of St Peter and when a sixth bell was added in 1810 the name was not changed. Here, in 1783, was formed the Chailey Friendly Society, the oldest friendly society in Sussex. Its object was 'to raise money by subscription of members to be applied to their relief and maintenance in sickness, old age and infirmity, and also to the relief of their widows.'

On 4th June every year the society held its annual meeting and this took the form of a feast day which was celebrated as a general holiday throughout the parish.

SWAN INN: This 17th century inn later became the property of the Shiffner family of Coombe Place and was let, with a farm, to a tenant landlord. One such landlord was noted for his stews which he cooked in a huge cauldron over the fire in the bar parlour. One cold day, according to local recollection, the stew smelled particularly good but as he ladled it out something dark and woolly appeared on the spoon. 'Well, I'll be danged' he is reported to have said. 'I wondered where that old sock had got to.'

Shortly before the First World War, when the Shiffners had let Coombe Place and were living at Beven Bridge House, they would have guests to stay for the hunting and occasionally some young bachelors among them would be put up at the Swan. One of these young men was author and war poet Siegfried Sassoon and he based some of his *Memoirs of a Foxhunting Man* on the Swan and his days out with hounds from there.

KING'S HEAD: A petition signed by 43 people, including a churchwarden and two parish overseers, asked the justices to renew the licence of these premises as a 'common victualling house' in October 1649. It appears from the details of the application that the widow of the previous licence holder, Ralph Smallfield, had quickly remarried and wished to carry on the business with her new partner.

The petitioners – 'Thomas Hooke and his wife, Ann' – put forward a good case. Their dwellinghouse, they said, being the sign of the Kings Head in the road from Lewes to London, has all the conveniences of house room and otherwise for the entertainment of passengers, both horse and foot. 'And your petitioner, Ann, used to baking of bread for poor people who cannot buy their own corn, they humbly desire your worships would be pleased to continue their licence. ... as formerly so long as they keep good order.'

The 'hereunto subscribed inhabitants of Chailey' certified that the house of Hooke 'is a very fit and convenient house not only to entertaining passengers but for public meetings of the county'. They also agreed that 'the said Ann while she be the wife of Ralph Smallfield (who once kept the said house in his lifetime) and since hath always behaved herself soberly and discreetly and that there be no house in our parish so fit for entertainment'.

CHALVINGTON

YEW TREE: This village inn has its own cricket ground which is first documented in 1836. Twelve years earlier there was mention of a cricket pitch at the adjoining village of Ripe which had its own team in 1762 when it played Arlington at the Dicker Fair on 6th July.

Ripe and Chalvington combined their teams in 1826 and

played against the Cliffe, Lewes on Cliffe Hill, winning by 45 runs. Two players who later played for the county side turned out for Chalvington when they entertained Brighton on the Yew Tree ground. They are brothers George and Robert Picknell, both of whom are buried in the churchyard.

Before cricket, smuggling was the name of the game at the Yew Tree. A landlord of the late 18th, early 19th century William Henty was a great gambler and often a lucky one. Repeatedly he would wager on this and that with the free traders and more often than not win quantities of contraband from them. But once luck went against him. He wagered the deeds of the pub on the turn of a card – and lost. He too, is buried in Chalvington churchyard.

CHIDDINGLY

SIX BELLS: A happy, if unusual marriage – and a murder. Rightly this inn can claim all human life was here. The marriage was between the first owner, a Mrs Grey, who at the age of 60 married a man aged 26. He proudly announced that he had achieved his life's ambition of marrying a woman who was deaf and dumb – and owned a pub.

The murder came later. On 7th January 1852 a farm labourer called French died after being unwell for some days. The jury at the inquest held at the Six Bells returned a verdict of death by natural causes but tongues began to wag. A few weeks later the widow, Sarah Anne French was arrested and the body exhumed. There was another inquest at the inn and this time the jury's verdict, announced by the foreman, the vicar the Rev James Vidal, was wilful murder by Sarah Anne.

The case, when it came to trial, became known as the Onion Pie Murder. On Christmas Eve 1851 French told a fellow worker William Funnell that he was going to have an onion pie for his supper. He was ill for the next few days and when he returned to work he told another friend that he thought his wife was carrying on with their lodger, young James Hickman.

Hickman admitted to such a liaison when he gave evidence at Lewes Assizes and also said that he told Sarah he would marry her if her husband died.

Sarah, before her trial, told a magistrate that Hickman had put arsenic in the onion pie, but at Lewes she confessed only to buying arsenic from the wife of a farrier at Horsebridge 'to kill some rats'. The jury found her guilty of murder and she was sentenced to death. She was the last woman to be hanged publicly at Lewes and there was a crowd of between 3,000 and 4,000 people in North Street and on Brack Mount to watch the sentence being carried out in Hangman's Acre.

After the execution the prison chaplain said that Sarah had admitted killing her husband. She had not put the arsenic in the onion pie but had administered it 'in a way not desirable to mention'.

CROWBOROUGH

CROWBOROUGH CROSS HOTEL: The present premises date from the 17th century when this was the Red Cross Inn but there was an earlier wooden building on the site which was an alehouse in the 16th century. At least four coaches a week clattered past its doors in the 18th/19th centuries and that is how it got the name Red Cross Inn. There were no road maps in those days and the coachmen had to find their way with the help of 3 inch wide drawings of the road only, which they would rotate on rollers as they went along. Each stage would have a symbol on these routes and the Crowborough crossroads were marked with a red cross.

The interior of the inn has been altered considerably since its coaching days but there is still ample evidence of its historic past.

Here, in the 1960s, was a coincidental meeting between a pre First World War landlord and a representative of Charrington's brewery. Mr John Hamblyn now the surveyor for the brewery, and then a junior representative, called to inspect the pub's boiler which was giving a bit of trouble. He was introduced to 93 year old Charles Deverall and his daughter who had dropped in for lunch. 'Mr Deverall, who held the licence from 1905, had never met anyone from the brewery before' said Mr Hamblyn. 'In course of conversation he said that in those days the landlord of the Cross had the funeral rites from Crowborough to Bexhill and was also the head of the volunteer fire brigade.' At this point the then licensee produced some old photographs showing Mr Deverall and some firemen putting out a fire in the roof of the inn.

DITCHLING

B ULL INN: In the 1790s a regular coach from London to Brighton via Lindfield and Ditchling called here to change horses. And some years later, in the early days of newspapers when they cost 5d the villagers would gather at the inn to hear the local schoolmaster read the local news to them.

Grouse suppers were held here, and tripe and onion suppers, and the Ditchling Currant and Gooseberry Show, and the Kettle Feast and Stoolball match at which the Southdown Band from Poynings played while officials and press representatives had dinner.

The Bull also had its own club. Every Whit Monday the members met at 10am at the inn and proceeded to the vicarage to collect the vicar and escort him to church. After a service there would be a lavish lunch at the Bull and the afternoon would be spent as a gala day.

WHITE HART: At 4am on a day in October 1806 the licensee Mr Harnott was disturbed by a noise. He went to investigate and disturbed two men, one of whom drew a pistol on him. Harnott tackled the man and got him by the hair. The other intruder got away. Mr Harnott had caught a known murderer and smuggler, Robert Bignall and his accomplice John Tingley was later captured by Mr Gatland, the landlord of the Swan at Chailey. Both Bignall and Tingley had escaped from Rochester goal where they were awaiting trial for robbery. At Horsham they were charged with burglary and stealing 31 shillings in cash, a watch and other articles. Bignall was sentenced to death and a crowd of 3,000 watched his execution. Tingley was acquitted.

There is no mention of any reward for the innkeepers who apprehended the villains.

EASTBOURNE

LAMB INN: This former church house was converted to an inn at the time of the Reformation. Sussex historian Mark Anthony Lower described it as 'probably one of the oldest houses of entertainment in the county' with a crypt or vaulted cellar in the Early English style. The premises have been considerably altered since Lower visited them in 1858 when they were owned by a fellow member of the Sussex Archaeological Society William Harvey. There was some particularly heavy restoration in 1912 when the building was covered with white painted stucco. A postcard showing the inn as it looked in those days is in the town's local history collection and then there was not a sign of the many beams that cover the exterior today.

In 1761 the Lamb required a new tenant. An announcement in the *Sussex Weekly Advertiser* in November of that year described it as 'an ancient accustomed inn, to which always has been good, and now is exceeding good trade'. The household furniture and stock of liquors were available to the person taking the inn at an ingoing price of £4,000 and inquirers were referred to the Widow Keeys at the Lamb.

In the Napoleonic wars, when the town was full of soldiers, the Lamb was the centre of social life. Many lavish balls were held there and the *Globe* of 9th September 1809 reported that 'all the officers of the 2nd Surrey and Shropshire Regiments with that politeness that distinguishes these gentlemen, send their bands every evening for the amusement of the company.'

Later on there were more serious gatherings in the inn's meeting room. In May 1852 Dr Darling gave a lecture on such occult subjects as spiritualism, table turning and Mesmerism. During the proceedings there was a tremendous thunderstorm of such violence that the audience was convinced that it was a manifestation of Satan. Some of the less stout-hearted ran from the room.

One landlord of the Lamb was Thomas Picknell, brother of Sussex cricketers George and Robert Picknell. Another was Eli Thomas Silvester who had a token struck bearing the inscription 'Lamb Hotel, Eastbourne. T.B. Silvester. 3d.' Eli Thomas appears in Kelly's Directory of 1882 as landlord at the Lamb. His token was found not all that long ago by a man with a metal detector working over a deeply ploughed field at Birling Manor, East Dean.

CROWN INN: Miller Thomas Hurst was said to have lifted a young and truculent gipsy on the palm of one hand and crashed him through the ceiling of the pub's bar. Another person to come into painful contact with the structure was Dr Alexander Brodie who died in 1828 when he was thrown from his carriage against a wall of the Crown.

ALBION HOTEL: Originally built as a guest house but it failed to attract enough customers and in 1852 it was bought by the Earl of Ashburnham as a seaside home for his children. But he did not have the words 'guest house' quite painted out from the exterior wall and on one occasion he was not at all pleased to find a stranger on the premises. He got even more annoyed when the stranger called to him: 'Waiter, bring me some sherry please.'

The Albion reverted to hotel status around the turn of the century and acquired a reputation for comfort and service when it was run by Alderman James Rudd.

TALLY HO: This fine example of brewers' building has now acquired as much ornamentation outside as it has inside. It was built around the turn of the century and its façade then proudly bore the inscription: 'Frank Boorer, Lion Brewery, Ales and Stout'. It had its pillars and arches but not the present entrance, up steps from the corner of Church Street and Green Street, and decorated with a coloured frieze of huntsmen and hounds.

In the red plush and mahogany interior with its saloon and lounge bars and a separate pool room there are a number of blown up picture postcards of Eastbourne as it was in the early 20th century. There is a particularly interesting one of the nearby Lamb Inn. It shows a white painted rendered building – with not a single beam in sight, and a sign painted on the road frontage reading: 'Historical Lamb Hotel. W.F. Walton. Wines and Spirits, A Bottled Beer Merchant. Bass and Co., Pale and Burton Ales, Celebrated London Stout. Special Scotch and Irish Whiskies. Good Stabling.'

NEW INN: Thomas Fuller, licensee here from around 1752, was an early entrepreneur of road transport and a believer in the power of advertising. He ran a coach from Eastbourne to Lewes during the summer months and for some 25 years he advertised its departure and arrival times – and kept to them. In March and April he would say that Fuller's coach would run until further notice, and in November he would announce that the service would stop until further notice.

In 1804 Thomas Fuller announced that a diligence would leave for Brighton at 9am on Mondays, Wednesdays and Fridays and return on alternate days. As far as he was concerned the customer was always right. He introduced a new route to the coast via Uckfield but also put on a coach to take the route via Lewes so his passengers could choose which way they wished to go. So successful was this enterprise that Thomas Fuller was able to refurbish the inn from the profits he made.

On 16th December 1800 a Society for Prosecuting Thieves, Felons and Receivers of Stolen Goods was formed at the New Inn.

BUCCANEER: This pub was built in 1897 as the Devonshire Park Hotel by the Devonshire Park and Baths Company. It was designed by architect Henry Ward of Hastings who had been inspired by the Indian Pavilion built for an exhibition of the P & O Line later brought to Eastbourne as a tea pavilion in the park. It was demolished in the 1960s to make way for the Congress Theatre.

EAST CHILTINGTON

JOLLY SPORTSMAN: This former cottage alehouse has been altered and extended to cope with the demand for its facilities. Without it the East Chiltingtonians would have nowhere to meet for they sold their village hall in the 1960s because it did not pay. The site went for housing and the cash realised went to the church funds. Now the parish council, all seven members of it, meet in the pub when there are matters to discuss and every time there is an election the polling station is in a room there. One year, when an election inconveniently occurred when there was a change of licensee, the room was not available and the electorate of 293 had to make their way to a barn to cast their votes.

Until quite recently a room at the pub was also the village shop but when trade fell away to a trickle it was closed down.

The building was formerly thatched and is still known, to the older inhabitants, as 'the Thatch'.

EAST HOATHLY

KINGS HEAD: In May 1761 'at the house of John Jones a
main of cocks was held between the gentlemen of
Hoathly and the gentlemen of Pevensey showing nine cocks a
side for two guineas a battle and ten guineas the odd battle.'
It was in premises in front of the Kings Head that Henry
Rich set up as a manufacturer of chairs and trugs when he was
24 years of age. That was in 1810 and he died in 1867. His
tombstone is in the south wall of the tower of the church of
which he was clerk and sexton for 57 years. Henry Rich's
business was continued until 1956, making hoops and all kinds
of wooden goods. He presented a trug to Queen Victoria at
the Great Exhibition in 1851. It would not have cost much to
manufacture as a good workman could turn out some five
dozen trugs a week, as well as an assortment of handles and
rakes.

FALMER

SWAN INN: In 1828 an agreement was drawn up at this
inn between sheep shearers and the farmers for whom
they worked. Chairman was John Ellman, great Sussex sheep
breeder and agricultural expert, and various points were
agreed.
The men were to be at work at 7am and there would be cold
meat or meat pies for their breakfast and one quart of ale per
man. They were to light up their pipes twice in the forenoon
and be allowed each time one pint of ale. Dinner was to consist

of boiled meat and half a pint of small beer with and after the meal. Twice in the afternoon they could light up and have half a pint of mixed beer – half ale, half strong ale – the first time and the other half of the pint on the second occasion. There would be cold meats for supper and one quart of ale and a pint of strong beer per man. They would be allowed 1½ hours for supper and to drink their beer but no smoking or singing was allowed.

The old Swan Inn where this agreement was signed, sometimes with crosses sometimes with names, was near the almshouses. The present inn was built when the road was straightened after the Second World War.

FIRLE

RAM INN: Petty sessions were held in this inn and on one occasion, in 1839, three magistrates were on the bench. A message was brought to one of them saying that there was someone below who wished to speak to him. He went down and had a writ served on him and was told he was under arrest and that he should send for another magistrate if he wanted bail. He sent the necessary message by the court usher and the second magistrate turned up and was also arrested. The third member of the bench was summoned to bail the first two out – and he also received a writ. Then they bailed each other out and returned to their magisterial duties. One of the three magistrates, all of whom were dunned for debt, was Sir William Carr of Beddingham.

Firle originally had four pubs, the Polecat, the Ram, the Woolpack and the Beanstalk but in 1812 the old turnpike road was closed in favour of a new road to Eastbourne and Firle found itself at the end of a cul-de-sac, with disastrous results on trade.

But the village continued to play cricket. All day matches against Falmer and Stanmer Cricket Club were regular fixtures and Viscount Gage once played for the village team. Lunch was served at the Ram when Sam Mockett was the landlord and the tables would be gay with flowers and a splendid repast costing 2s 6d was provided. The games were played on the field near the inn and there was not much high scoring as there was too much grass in the outfield.

FLETCHING

ROSE AND CROWN INN: In January 1626, according to the Sussex Quarter Sessions Records for that year, John Parsons was granted a licence to keep an alehouse in Fletching. He entered into a £20 bond and undertook to keep and maintain good order and rule in his house and not to suffer 'any drunkenness or any unlawful games ... or to suffer suspected persons or of evil living to his knowledge to lodge in the said house'.

The alehouse is not named. Perhaps it was this wattle and daub house which dates from the reign of King Stephen, around 1150. Successive restorations have not totally expunged the original building materials and a sample of the early wattle and daub, taken from a rear wall during 1939 alterations, has been preserved. In 1874 the landlord had the Old Testament name of Abednego Weston. He was succeeded by his son Joseph who was helped in the pub by his sister Faith. She kept cats and always wore a long cloak and a bonnet when she walked about the village.

Bread was brought by horse and trap from Whitesides at Uckfield and put out on a scrubbed wooden table in the public bar for people to collect. Another member of the family, Ben Weston, would deliver loaves on a handcart to customers who could not, or would not, collect their own. Ben was noted for turning up at church on Sundays with a beef steak pudding wrapped in a red and white spotted handkerchief.

GRIFFIN INN: The only conveyance to Fletching from the nearest railway station at Sheffield Park in the 1880s was a waggonette belonging to the landlord Mr George Stevenson, who also ran a thriving coal and coke business. He charged his passengers 7s 6d for the round trip – taking them to the station in time to catch the morning train and collecting them from the down train in the evening.

FOREST ROW

THE SWAN: These premises were used for the sale of alcohol by the widow Mary Martin in 1750 and later on her son, Richard, paid a hen a year to the Lord of the Manor for the tenancy. The type of hen – whether pullet, broody or a good laying bird – is not stipulated in the agreement. Richard Martin was licensed to sell liquor at the Yew Tree Inn and it was still called by that name when it was visited by the Honourable John Byng in 1788. He reported that he had called 'at the right kind of house and at the right time too. A leg of mutton just boiled added to a plumb pie, with a good cheese, and a half a pint of brandy made me feel as full as an alderman.'

Charles Abbott, Speaker of the House of Commons, who had moved into Kidbroke Park in 1802, bought the inn when the licensee, William Langridge was having money troubles. Langridge was allowed to stay on as tenant on condition that he cleared his outstanding debts but this he failed to do. In 1805 he received a letter from Mr Speaker's solicitor. 'Pay the

£500 you owe or get out' it said. Langridge got out and a few months later John Hoare applied for and was granted a licence for the Swan at the licensing sessions held at Sheffield Park. He had been butler to a branch of the De La Warr family and ran the inn with professional efficiency for 30 years. He ended up as an old man on crutches and suffering from gout, as a pensioner in Sackville College, East Grinstead, but he had made the Swan the social centre of Forest Row.

It was John Hoare who started a local annual sports day. The first one, held on 25th June 1826, featured racing, dancing, jumping, juggling and other rural pleasures and ended with a magnificent fireworks display. The inn has recently been extensively modernised.

BRAMBLETYE: This inn was opened in the 1870s when the East Grinstead to Groombridge railway line connected Forest Row by rail to London and Tunbridge Wells.

But its greatest claim to fame was that Sir Arthur Conan Doyle, who lived in Crowborough, wrote a Sherlock Holmes tale *Black Peter* and set it in the Brambletye Inn which no doubt he visited on a number of occasions.

GLYNDE

TREVOR ARMS: The year before the railway came to Glynde this pub was built to receive its customers. Its site in Pick Field was leased from Lord Hampden in 1845 and the old village pub, part of which became the post office, closed down. It, like its predecessor which was on a site now occupied by Rosemary and Rambler Cottages, was on the old road from Ringmer. The new road, past the present Trevor Arms, is relatively modern.

The new inn was a Harvey's house from the start. In 1845 Mr H O Trevor leased it to John Harvey, wine merchant of Cliffe, Lewes, for 21 years, at an annual rental of £4 10s. In 1863 a 24 year lease was negotiated between the Hon H W Brand and William and Henry Harvey of Lewes Brewery at a reduced rental – only £2 5s.

The pub was extended in 1929 and the new room, now the barn bar, became the headquarters of the Glynde and Beddingham Cricket Club which celebrated its centenary in 1985.

The inn sign shows the arms of the Trevor family. Sir John Trevor was Secretary of State and Privy Councillor to Charles II. He married Ruth, daughter of Sir John Hampden. The fourth Lord Trevor assumed the name and arms of Hampden in 1776. A later member of the family was Henry Bouverie Brand, Speaker of the House of Commons and MP for Lewes from 1852.

GROOMBRIDGE

VICTORIA INN: This village alehouse started life as part of three toll cottages and travellers going to and from Old Groombridge along the Withyham road had to pay a toll of 2d at the gate – and they had no choice. However, there was an alternative route through the miller's field for people going from the station to Old Groombridge. They could bypass the toll but had to pay a penny to the miller Caleb Russell, or his brother Isaac, to do so. The penny they had saved they often spent on ale at the inn.

In the Second World War anti-aircraft guns were stationed in the inn yard but later transferred to the top of Groombridge Hill.

GUESTLING

WHITE HART: Jumping down wells or hanging oneself in stables or haylofts were favourite forms of self-destruction in the 17th and 18th centuries. Then there were no barbiturates on which to overdose or carbon monoxide to inhale from a car's exhaust, and only a few people were in walking distance of Beachy Head. Ebenezer Ramsey, licensee of this inn from 1874 until 1888 chose to hang himself in the stables at the rear of the premises. But he lives on in effigy – and for charity. A model has been made of him and it is seated in the cellar with a bottle of beer in one hand and a glass in the other. He can be viewed through a grille and customers are encouraged to throw down onto the display money which is collected and distributed regularly to local charities. Perhaps poor Ebenezer's desperate act may ultimately do someone some good.

HADLOW DOWN

NEW INN: There was a New Inn here in the early 1800s but it was burned down in the 1880s and there were rumours that the fire did not start accidentally. Perhaps they were started because at the time of the blaze the bailiffs were attempting to distrain upon the possessions of the landlord who had inconveniently run out of cash and credit.

The New Inn today is next door to a scrapyard. Its opening hours can vary; it has only one useable door; there are three barrels on the bar and they all contain Harvey's pale ale – in perfect condition always. The local 'rockers' have laid claim to the back room. Here is living history. ...

HAILSHAM

CROWN HOTEL: There was a Crowne Inn in Hayleshame in 1632 when it was bequeathed by Nicholas Stonestreet to his brother Henry. Around 1770 it was converted into two shops and 200 years later one of the shops, run as a grocery business for many years, was demolished to make way for an extension of the National Westminster Bank. This demolition revealed the 16th century origins of the old Crowne. Over the fireplace was an oak bressummer beam with the design of a crown burned into it and an opening with a low pointed arch was uncovered, of a style popular in the reign of Elizabeth I.

The present Crown was leased in 1808 to Thomas Charlton, gentleman, of Loose, Kent and Richard Gibbs of Herstmonceux and they conveyed it to Brighton brewer William Wigney for £1,000. In 1850 Wigney conveyed it to Vallance and Catt, also Brighton brewers, and in 1885, after it had passed through a few more hands, a spirits merchant of Hailsham named Holland Southerden sold it to innkeeper John Butcher for £1,650.

From 1818 until a special room was built for them 80 years later, vestry meetings were held at the Crown and also at other inns in the area. The Corn Exchange flourished in a room at the rear and it was here, in 1849, a dinner was held to celebrate the opening of the Hailsham to Polegate railway line. It was a celebration marked by tragedy, for a young man, John Hield, was killed on the first journey. He was standing on the carriage footplate and was dragged off by the crossing gate at Mulbrook.

A character who brought colour to the respectable Crown

was town crier and auctioneer Ody Wenham who used to sell goods outside the inn on market days. On his rostrum he had a notice stating:

Ody Wenham begs to say
On every Hailsham market day,
He, being a licensed auctioneer,
He writes and takes in orders here.

GRENADIER HOTEL: A deed found in a chest in St Mary's parish church records that William Stevens of Berwick and J Worger of Alfriston were to build a house in the field of Benjamin Shelley near the barracks on Hailsham Common for the purpose of supplyng beer for use of the barracks. Mr Richard Wood, innkeeper, was to have a half share in the business.

The barracks were built in 1800 and occupied in succession by the South Gloucester Militia, the 23rd Regiment of Foot and the Dorset Militia, and the 8th Regiment of Foot. One of the famous athletes of the day (he walked 1,000 miles in 1,000 hours) was Captain Barclay of the 23rd Foot and he lodged in the town, but not at the British Grenadier as the pub was then called.

In 1811 the soldiers went away and so did most of Richard Wood's trade. He set out to attract a new sort of custom by offering to buy birds, particularly owls and hawks, for which he would pay 3d each. Soon his house was the local for every tramp in the area, some of them the soldiers that had once marched off to war with France from the barracks and now had to beg in the streets for a living.

A later war saw the premises used for a different purpose. Hailsham Evening Women's Institute met there in April 1940, and decided to resume their regular monthly programme of events which had been abandoned at the outbreak of the Second World War.

GEORGE HOTEL: An unfortunate mistake in the kitchens ruined the 25th anniversary dinner of the Hailsham Prosecuting Society in the early years of the 19th century. The inn was owned by Lewes brewer George Wood and the landlord was famous cricketer John Baker, who, with his cousin, gamekeeper James Bray, played for Sussex at Hawkhurst against a Kent side in 1816. Members of the society, all important men in the locality, started to tuck into the turkey which was always a feature of their dinners. But this time, although it had been drawn before it was roasted, its crop had been left in and the stuffing, usually a delicacy of the house, tasted dreadful and was of the consistency of crushed glass. The cook was called in and castigated and the society appointed five of its members to act as a vetting committee to inspect future turkeys while they were being prepared and cooked for the annual dinners.

Hailsham Petty Sessions were held at the George in the early 19th century. Two magistrates held court in the confined space of two upper rooms.

HARTFIELD

ANCHOR: Before it became an inn some 100 years ago this was a workhouse for women and in 1842 it was owned by the Rev Dr Rand's charity and was under the control of the Hartfield Board of Guardians. This control must have been pretty strict because in recent renovations ankle chains were discovered, presumably used to restrict the movements of the more wayward inmates.

In 1915 the Anchor was advertised in the parish magazine as an inn with 'private accommodation for small parties with carriages to meet trains by order'.

HAYWAGGON: In 1781, when it was called the Dorset Arms, this inn was owned by Hartfield victuallers Obadiah Elliott and Henry Edwards. Its name was not changed until the 1960s when it was sold by Earl de la Warr's estate.

Lodging there in 1820 was a Mr Artherfold who lost some money either at Hartfield or on the road to Hartwell and Lower Paddock on 24th July of that year between 4pm and 7pm. Posters were put up on notice boards in the village advertising a reward for the return of 'the sum of £6 by three £1 notes of the Lewes Old Bank, one of Taplin's Bank and one of Lashmar's Bank of Brighton together with one sovereign, the same folded up together. The numbers of the notes are known and the owner's private mark to each and the banks and shops in the neighbourhood have notice of it. Whoever will bring the same to Mr Artherfold at the Dorset Arms shall be handsomely rewarded for the same and any person keeping the same after this notice, will be prosecuted with the utmost rigour.'

The penalty for stealing by finding in those days was death. But there are no records of anyone being convicted so perhaps Mr Artherfold got his money back.

GALLIPOT INN: Three almshouses, built by the parish for its poor in the 16th century, were later occupied by three brothers. In one cottage lived Jack Sands who made shoes for the gentry and clogs for the workers; in another lived William who brewed beer and cider; and in the third lived Albert who made small, glazed jars called gallipots which were used for medicines. When his brothers died William converted all three cottages into one inn and it has been a free house ever since.

HASTINGS

CINQUE PORTS: One of the oldest inns in the town and formerly known as the Chequer. In 1642 Richard Tester paid a quitrent of 2s 6d for his tenement called the Chequer but 14 years later the premises were described as three houses and Tester's quitrent for his section was reduced to 1 shilling.

Some hundred years later the inn was known as the Old Chequer – which by then it was. The first time it appears in the records as the Cinque Ports is in 1824 when it was owned by William Wood who had paid £260 for it eight years previously.

STAG INN: There are some strange regulars in the main bar of this old inn – two mummified cats and a rat – and some strange games are played here.

The cats were found when the fireplace was opened up some 35 years ago. The rat arrived from somewhere else – but no one is prepared to say from where. The mummified cats have given rise to a splendid story, a printed copy of which, bearing the initials JM circulates freely among customers around closing time. Hastings was one of the earliest towns to have an air defence system, so the story goes. A local witch called Hannah Clarke would cruise the skies on her broomstick, with her two cats as pillion passengers, watching out for the French invaders and warning the populace when she spotted pirates. Her cats also kept the Old Town free of rats and everyone was happy. That was until 1662 when a hearth tax was imposed and the fireplace at the Stag bricked up to avoid the duty. Hannah had time to snatch up her broomstick from its resting place on the chimneypiece and make off for a safer base from which to conduct her aerial operations. But her cats were asleep on the hearth and were bricked up accidentally. They were rediscovered by a cat burglar in 1875....

The Stag's strange games were devised by regular customer Mark Pennington. What started him off was the reference to a game of 'loggetts' in the conditions attached to Thomas Stevenson the Younger's grant of a licence to keep a common alehouse and victualling house in 1603. Young Thomas was ordered 'not to suffer or permit or to have any playing at cards, dices, tables, quoits, loggetts, scailes, bowls or any other unlawful game or games ..' which finished off the game until Mark revived it in 1983.

It took him a lot of research and a lot of hard, physical work. He had to carve a mannikin wearing a top hat and with opposing faces – one smiling, the other downcast, and to make a hollow wooden ball to contain a length of line and nine wooden bowls of different shapes – three egg shaped, three tomato shaped and three potato shaped. The game is played out of doors and is a variation on bowls. The top hatted mannikin is thrown backwards over the shoulder of one of the competitors to decide who starts and where from. A peg with the wooden ball attached to it is then hammered into the ground at the spot where the mannikin fell and the object of the game is to throw the oddly shaped bowls as near to it as possible. The distance is measured by the line within the ball.

The other game played at the Stag is also a Mark Pennington invention and he holds the record of completing it – in 3 minutes 57 seconds. A pyramid of wooden squares have to be transferred from one of three pegs on a board to the third peg, using the middle peg as a staging post. The problem is that it is forbidden to have a smaller square above a larger one. It looks dead easy and is extremely difficult.

CROWN INN: This inn was the only real rival to the Swan as a coaching inn and centre of fashionable life in 18th and 19th century Hastings. The Swan has gone and its site is now laid out as gardens but the Crown continues. It was run by William Smith from 1794–1814 and by his widow, Sarah, from 1815 to 1832. It had extensive stables, reaching as far as Tackleway, and they were kept busy when the coaches called.

The Widow Smith received a commendation from *Powell's Guide to Hastings* of 1831. 'Mrs Smith deserves particular support, as being the first (with a family of seven children) to add to the accommodation of visitors' it states. This is done, according to the guide, 'by every species of comfort, neatness and domestic attention'.

ROYAL STANDARD: In 1707 a mariner, cordwainer, fisherman and boatbuilder owned this property and sold it in 1806 to another mariner John Nash. He passed it on, for a cash consideration, in 1822 to tapster Richard Piper and so it became a pub. Richard's eldest son, also called Richard, sold it in 1853 for £495 after his father had been lost at sea in the *Four Sisters*. The Star Brewery bought the pub in 1925 and it is now a Shepherd Neame house and serves tea and coffee as well as alcohol in the summer months.

HASTINGS ARMS: From 1794 until 1824 this inn remained in the family of John Sargent and a Grand Lodge of Druids was opened here in 1822. When some restoration work was being done in the 1960s a compartment was discovered under a window seat which had room for three barrels of ale, some of which were still in position, and piped to the cellars. Another three barrels were discovered under another window seat. Some sort of villainy must have been practised there. Perhaps the barrels contained untaxed liquors.

JENNY LIND: This pub was severely bombed in 1943 and has since been rebuilt so bears no resemblance to the Elizabethan house built on the site of the Bell Inn and sold to tallow chandler James Bachelor in 1613. It was opened as an inn by Robert Robinson in the 1850s.

HEATHFIELD

JACK CADE: Formerly called the Half Moon – its name was not changed until after the Second World War. In earlier days it was used as a courthouse for the petty sessions and was the scene of the Heffle Fair on 14th April each year. On fair days it was said that an old woman would let a cuckoo out

of her basket to herald the coming of spring. The land round the pub would be full of horses and cattle, gipsies showing off the ponies they had for sale, swings and roundabouts, stalls and coconut shies. Children would have a day off school and it was an occasion for general merriment, combined with a bit of business and plenty of beer.

Jack Cade who gave his name to Cade Street (it used to be Carter's or Cat's Street) was a wild Irishman who lead an insurrection in 1450, defeating the king's forces at Sevenoaks and marching on London with 30,000 men. His blaze of riot did not last and he was mortally wounded by an arrow from the bow of Alexander Iden, Sheriff of Kent, just outside Heathfield. This was a kind of poetic justice because Iden had replaced William Cromer whose execution Cade had ordered when he was in London.

Near the pub, at the place were Cade was captured, is a stone pillar put up by Francis Newbery, one time owner of Heathfield Park. It bears the inscription: 'Near this spot was slain the notorious rebel Jack Cade by Alexander Iden, Sheriff of Kent. AD 1450. His body was carried to London and his head fixed on Tower Bridge. This is the success of all rebels and this future chanceth ever to traitors.'

CROWN: The people of Heathfield are incredibly honest – or rather the patrons of this 1930s style roadhouse are. It is, if you will forgive me, a personal story. On a Bank Holiday Monday in 1983 I arranged to meet some friends in the Crown's car park and transfer deck chairs, food and bottles of wine to their car and go on with them to Heathfield Races. I took my purse out of my handbag to pay the £1 fee for an afternoon's parking and went to the races. When I got there I found I had not got my purse – which in one way was a good thing because I could not back any losers. When I was driven back to the Crown after the meeting I walked to my car and found my purse, full of cash and credit cards, sitting prominently on the top of the boot lid.

HELLINGLY

GOLDEN MARTLET: When the London, Brighton and South Coast Railway extended its line from Hailsham to Tunbridge Wells in 1880 a station was built at Hellingly, and a Station Hotel.

In the Second World War that small hotel was commandeered by the Army and personnel of the 21st General Hospital Unit of the Royal Army Medical Corps were billeted there. This unit went to France in February 1940, was brought off the beaches of Dunkirk, then re-equipped and sent to India. Nearby Hellingly Hospital was the headquarters for a succession of RAMC units, many members of which were quartered at the hotel.

When the railway closed in 1968 the station was turned into a private house and the track became the Cuckoo Walk, now so popular with ramblers and wildlife. The pub also got a new name.

HERSTMONCEUX

WOOLPACK INN: Agricultural unrest was at its height in Sussex around 1830. Gangs of farm labourers, their faces blackened, went from farm to farm at night setting fire to crops, machinery and hay barns. They were trying to draw attention to the fact that they had to work for near starvation wages, while the farmers and landowners grew richer and richer. The disturbances became known as the Swing riots, named after the Captain Swing pseudonym adopted by the writers of various letters threatening landowners with death and destruction unless something was done.

It was as a result of one such disturbance in Herstmonceux that the Riot Act was read from the steps of the Woolpack.

Meetings of a more peaceful nature took place at the inn in 1893 to consider the formation of a local fire brigade. Mr C S Arkoll said he would buy a manual fire engine from the Hailsham brigade for £30 if it was demonstrated and delivered. It was, and he did, and the Herstmonceux and Wartling Volunteer Fire Brigade was formed.

HOOE

LAMB INN: When the Abbot of Battle, Lawrence Champion, first granted a licence to this alehouse in 1510 he imposed a condition – that the premises should always be kept warm and, particularly during the lambing season, be kept open day and night in case shepherds needed to bring their sheep in from the cold. In those days the alehouse was surrounded by marshland on which the sheep grazed. It was not until 1929 that a new motor road was built across the marshes from Westham to Bexhill. Many of the workmen were unemployed miners from Wales, trying to earn a living in the Depression years.

RED LION: This was a smuggling inn, make no mistake about it. Its innkeeper was James Blackman, a member of the Groombridge gang, and he was the mastermind behind the convoys that moved contraband to the area of Ashdown Forest. In 1774 Jacobite James Bishop of Parham, his servant and James Ibbotson from Arundel sought Blackman's help when they were trying to escape to France, but he betrayed them.

Outside the inn were six lime trees, which were an indication to smugglers that this was a safe house. Inside it, attached to a beam in the attic was a machine for shredding tobacco. This would be transported wrapped between two strands of hempen rope and unwound and shredded for smoking at the inn. 'Money for old rope' they called it....

HORSEBRIDGE

KINGS HEAD: One of the earliest roads to be improved in Sussex stretched from Eastbourne to Uckfield via Horsebridge and Horam. A meeting of the trustees of the turnpike was held 'at the house of Armgill Terry, known as the Kings Head' in 1754 and a toll house was set up opposite the inn. As a road it flourished and by 1852 was one of only three in the county which had paid its way and was free from debt.

An aristocratic visitor clattered into the inn yard one day in 1788. It was the Honourable John Byng, a Lieutenant-Colonel in the Foot Guards and later to become the fifth Earl of Tortington. He kept an account of his travels round Sussex and of his visit to the Kings Head he said: 'My horse being put up and a double bedded room put into preparation (our luggage was arrived) the evening now closed we were soon at supper ... mutton chops, and boiled ham, in a sitting room of most spacious extent, being 36 feet by 21 feet. Our bedroom too was of noble dimensions...'

HOVE

SHIP HOTEL: A childhood prank almost destroyed this old inn in 1749. The *Gentlemen's Magazine* for that year reported that on 30th September the landlord's young son was playing when he found some gunpowder in a cupboard. The foolish child set a trail of it across the floor and set light to it. The explosion blew part of the back of the house to pieces, seriously injured two soldiers who were lodging there and left the boy with 'one eye destroyed and his body frightfully mutilated'.

The Ship was rebuilt in 1809 and 50 years later it was bought by Brighton brewer Henry Willett, who altered and extended it.

In the 18th century it was often the scene of cock fights and bull baits. There was a bull ring nearby and it was here, in 1810, that a baited bull escaped from its tether and charged the crowd. It was recaptured and baited to death by dogs.

IRON DUKE: When it opened in 1828 this inn was called the Kerrison Arms after Sir Edward Kerrison who served with the Duke of Wellington at Waterloo. He lived at Wick House from 1818 to 1825 and then moved to Brunswick Terrace.

First licensee was James Ireland who had been responsible for developing some pleasure gardens in Brighton which he hoped would rival Vauxhall. But they did not prove to be as successful as he had hoped so he took on the Kerrison Arms and also the job of collecting Hove's rates. He had to put up a £200 surety before his appointment was confirmed and he was paid 2½ per cent of the total amount he collected. When he died in 1842 the rate collecting job was amalgamated with that of town surveyor.

In 1910 the name of the inn was changed to the Hove Lawns Hotel in an attempt to attract a residential trade. In recent years it has reverted to its Waterloo connections. In 1974 the name was changed to the Iron Duke – this time the commanding officer rather than one of his subordinates.

ECLIPSE: There is no doubt about the date of this Victorian pub, 1886 is clearly marked on the western elevation. And there is no doubt about its connection with the turf. On one of the gables on the seaward side is a painted plaque of the famous thoroughbred after which the house is named, and on the other is *Diamond*, who ran over the Beacon course in the 1790s for a 300 guineas prize – and lost. Win one, lose one was perhaps the message the artist was intending to convey. Certainly *Eclipse* was a winner. Lord Grosvenor offered £11,000 for him after he had won the King's Plate for the 11th time.

Diamond was beaten by *Hambledonian* in his big race and he was not added to the pub's frontage until it was bought by Brighton brewers Vallance and Catt around the turn of the century.

ICKLESHAM

Q UEENS HEAD: The history of this inn has been framed in the bar for all to see. It was originally two farm tenements and ale was sold for the first time from the premises in April 1831 when pork butcher William Goodwin was in charge. He was succeeded by Rye butcher Frederick Sawkins who also combined the purveying of beef and beer.

It was not until the Star Brewery bought the premises in 1853 that it became known as the Queens Head. Another butcher took the tenancy in 1905. John Merritt was behind the bar pulling pints for part of the day and behind the counter of the adjoining butcher's shop cutting meat for the rest of his working hours. Not until the 1930s were the pub and the shop combined and the butchery side of the business abandoned.

When retired actor Anthony Crundell bought the freehold of the Queens Head from Courage who had bought it from the Star Brewery, it was said that the ghost of former landlord John Gutsell, who had died there in 1919, made the occasional reappearance. The apparition was seen in 1958 by a retired nurse from Bexhill, according to Jack Hallam's *Haunted Inns of England*.

Six years ago there was a fire at the inn and it was badly damaged. It has since been carefully restored and John Gutsell's ghost has not been seen again....

JEVINGTON

EIGHT BELLS: Any connections between this house, which became an inn after 1800 and the notorious smuggler Jevington Jigg who was sentenced to death at Salisbury in 1799 for horse stealing, was underground. In the 1790s it was a private house but there were passages from it, one leading to Thorpe House and another to a house called Jiggs. This could have been the home of James Pettitt, alias Jevington Jigg, and where he entertained the local villains.

It was during one such party, at which the 'ladies and gentlemen' were playing cards that the place was surrounded by eight or nine well armed policemen. One of the 'ladies' was greatly agitated and nearly fainted. She was allowed to pass through the police cordon to recover in the fresh air

whereupon she quickly cast off her bonnet and gown and fled. Jevington Jigg got away on that occasion but on 13th February 1790 he was discovered hiding in the roof of his house and taken to the House of Correction at Battle. He engaged a convincing counsel and was acquitted of obstructing the police and horse stealing. He was again acquitted, this time on a technical point, for horse stealing in 1792 but in 1793 he spent 18 months in Horsham jail before wangling a Royal pardon for stealing two sides of bacon. In April 1796 a jury found him not guilty of stealing hay and at Kent Assizes a charge of highway robbery was quashed.

It was not until he moved to Salisbury that his legal luck ran out – but not totally for his death sentence was commuted to 14 years' transportation.

In 1747 the house that later became the Eight Bells was willed by Edward Pearce to his nephew Richard. In 1780 it was bought by a Lewes banker for £2,500 and quickly sold to Edward Cooper for £2,800. A 'messuage and two gardens' were sold in 1800 to John Kine of Jevington, described as a victualler and he sold it a year later to Joseph Seymour, a labourer. Ten years later, Seymour, now described as a victualler, sold the part he had bought for £600 to John Gorring, a brewer of Seaford who immediately granted Seymour a seven year lease and the property became known as the Eight Bells. Why this name was chosen is not clear. The church of St Andrew at Jevington has only two bells in its tower.

LEWES

WHITE HART: The French Revolution and the American War of Independence owe something to this inn which until the early years of the 18th century was the town house of the Pelham family. It was here that Thomas Paine, author of *Common Sense*, *The Rights of Man* and *Age of Reason*, attended meetings of the Headstrong Club and he often won the Headstrong Book, an old Greek Homer, which was given each morning to the most obstinate debater of the previous night. After a spell as a rather unsuccessful Excise officer, during which time he lived at Bull House and married his landlord's daughter, Paine emigrated to America and wrote his pamphlet *Common Sense* in favour of American independence. He wrote his *Age of Reason*, an attack on Christianity, and advocating power to the people, in a Paris prison. His opinions were welcomed by the revolutionaries during the Reign of Terror. The Headstrong Club has been recently revived and meets again regularly at the White Hart.

Paine is by no means the only politician to visit this inn. In October 1929 in the same room in which the founder members of the Headstrong Club met in 1768, the then Foreign Secretary, Arthur Henderson, had a secret meeting with M Dovgalevsky, the Soviet Ambassador in Paris, to discuss the resumption of diplomatic relations between their respective governments.

Prime Minister Stanley Baldwin made a joking reference to this meeting during a debate in the House of Commons: 'In the old days I used to know the White Hart in Lewes very well' he said. 'To those whom it may interest I may say that you get the best of ale there. It is a great resort of people playing cricket in Sussex and, if I may use a simile which honourable members will all understand, that whereas the Foreign Secretary in July was playing with a straight bat very correctly and looked like keeping up his wicket, after lunch at the White Hart with M Dovgalevsky he was bowled out.'

John Byng was not quite so complimentary when he was here in 1788. 'Only good thing of novelty to us was some brill fish' he wrote. 'We were much displeased at the difficulty of getting an eating room and a double bedded sleeping room up two pairs of stairs but our fish at dinner was a treat and we ate of it with pleasure.'

Perhaps these were the same stairs that caused Mr and Mrs Sleigh to postpone their departure in October 1797. In the

Sussex Weekly Advertiser of 7th October Mr Sleigh informed the nobility and gentry of Lewes that 'in consequence of an unlucky fall from the top to the bottom of a stone flight of steps which Mrs Sleigh experienced on Thursday evening after a concert' they would stay on in Lewes longer than intended. 'A few friends have kindly undertaken to patronise a ball on October 10 at the White Hart' continues Mr Sleigh. 'In the course of the evening Mrs Sleigh will, if sufficiently recovered, sing several songs.'

During some alterations in 1907 a Tudor mantelpiece and some Tudor panelling were discovered and the inn's cellars come into the dungeon category.

ROYAL OAK: This alehouse on the steep hill leading up to the High Street started off as the White Horse but its name was changed around 1814 when John Pendrell became the licensee. He was the grandson of Dr Charles Pendrell, then a doctor living at Alfriston and a lineal descendant of the Pendrell brothers who hid Charles II after his defeat at the Battle of Worcester.

When Charles got his throne back he showed his gratitude to all who had helped him on his flight to France. He gave the Pendrells an annuity of 100 marks a year and the right of free warren (hunting whenever and wherever they chose) in perpetuity. Dr Charles Pendrell had inherited this annuity and always insisted, whenever he was godfather to a patient's child, that it should be called Charles – if it was a boy, of course. He also encouraged his family to continue the royal connection and, as several of them went into the licensed trade, they all changed the name of their inns to Royal Oaks.

LEWES ARMS: When John Spilsbury, the innkeeper, died in November 1773 he made precise arrangements for his own funeral. The *Sussex Weekly Advertiser* reported: 'On Wednesday evening last died John Spilsbury, master of the Lewes Arms public house in this town in which he acquired an ample fortune. A few years before his death he sent for a carpenter and gave him an order for making his coffin; he also named six publicans whom he desired might bear his remains to the grave, which were deposited yesterday evening at St John's churchyard.'

A later licensee incurred the displeasure of John Holman, High Constable of Lewes, by allowing his customers to drink on Sundays at the time of morning service.

On 28th October 1813 John Holman was called to the pub to quell a riot between some Irishmen from the 37th Regiment of Foot, then stationed at Hastings, and two porters from the coal yard and some Lewes residents. The outcome of this affray did not please Mr Holman. In his diary he complained bitterly that the magistrates only ordered the soldiers to pay 2s 6d each to one of the men they had hit. 'This is a good precedent for a constable, to go at all calls, amongst bayonets and swords, at the risk of his life, to make Peace by night and day' he wrote. 'These three fighting men are to be sent to their regiment and when arrived there all is to be hush, no man's character impeached unless the cut heads and black eyes should lead to any impertinent questions...'

On 14th November Mr Holman was in trouble again. He found a smith called George Wyatt intoxicated outside the inn and took him prisoner intending to put him in the lock-up. Then he found he had not got the key and, while waiting for it to be brought, he was attacked by Wyatt, who somehow fell and cut his head. Constable Holman then had to take his badly bleeding prisoner into the Lewes Arms and send for a doctor. 'We left him there and pursued our regular perambulations after giving Norman the landlord a severe reprimand whose house, (independent of this transaction) was disorderly' he records. 'Several persons being tippling therein during Divine Service, on our approach to do our duty, were permitted to hide themselves upstairs.'

The old inn was pulled down and rebuilt in its present form in 1823 and some 20 years later Brack Mount appears to have been annexed to the premises as a tea garden with 'summer houses, amusing games and ornamental trees and shrubs,' according to advertisements of the day. These al fresco activities had to stop when the Mount was bought in 1937 by Mrs Henry Dudeney.

DORSET ARMS: Some informers who were making life even more miserable for the Dissenters of the Cliffe lodged at this inn in 1670 but when they brought back goods they had seized from their victims the landlord threw them out. An account of what happened is in an appendix to Horsfield's *History of Lewes*. It sets out 'late proceedings of some justices and others pretending to put in execution the late Act against Conventicles against several peaceable people about the town of Lewes 1670.'

Of the informers it says: 'They thought to have lodged their spoils at the sign of the Cats in the Cliff but the master of the house (though no fanatick) said he would let no such goods come within his Doors, which made them take up quarters at another place'. The 'sign of the Cats' was the coat of arms of the Earls of Dorset which had two leopards as supporters. To people not familiar with the leopard – and few 17th century Englishmen were – they looked quite like cats with spots on.

Another customer who was asked to leave was horse thief Stephen Birstley, described as a 'servant to a farmer in Kent'. He stayed about 10 days at the Cats and aroused a certain amount of suspicion 'but by his fair pretences he was dismissed before the owner could come'.

In the 18th century the inn became a local centre for entertainment. It was visited on a couple of occasions by Mr and Mrs Astley with their 'learned horses'. One of the horses would 'sit up like a dog' and on others 'Master Griffiths, a boy of 14 years rides ... in many pleasing attitudes'.

There must have been a proper auditorium at the inn because a handbill announcing performances by Signor Marco's troupe from Italy charges for admission were: 'Pit 1s; first gallery 6d; upper gallery 4d.'

Prices were a little lower, 6d, 4d and 3d for 'curious experiments of the Camera Obscura, performed by John Pallany, an Italian, with variety of music on the Italian Cymbal.'

Audiences for these entertainments, which were usually held at 12 noon and 4pm, could come by coach for the Safety from Brighton called daily. When the railway came to Lewes carriers plied from the innyard forsaken by the coaches, going regularly to Brighton, Uckfield, Newhaven, Hailsham, Seaford and the villages between.

Like the rest of this part of the Cliffe the Dorset Arms suffered in the 1960s until a decision was made on the rerouting of the road. It was sold as a free house and, after the tunnel was built, re-opened under a different name – the Manxman. It sold again in the 1980s – to Harvey and Sons, whose Lewes brewery on the banks of the Ouse is only a few hundred yards away.

The Pelham Arms

PELHAM ARMS: There is some doubt about exactly when these premises first became an alehouse. If they were once called the Rose, as seems likely, they were flourishing in 1624, according to the diary of John Rowe, steward to Lord Bergavenny from 1597 to 1622 (SRS Vol 34). The entry reads: 'Eliz Machin vid p tento voc' le Rose g Hiders 17d.'

The churchwarden's accounts of St Anne's church, almost opposite the inn, refers to it in 1747 as the Dog. That entry reads: 'Town Constable paid one guinea for inquest of ye body of a soldier in Capt Burgen's Troop who shot himself at ye signe of ye Dogge'.

It was around 1790 that the name was changed to the Pelham Arms but nine years later the Earl of Chichester sold it to innkeeper Richard Williams, so severing the Pelham connection. Williams was clerk to Lewes racecourse until his death in 1821 so naturally the sporting fraternity of the town gathered at his inn. Its extensive stables were used by the local trainers and the stallion *Fearnought*, by the *Godolphin Arabian*, was at stud here before he was sent to America. In 1870 Thomas Read, a retired jockey, was the licensee and many famous figures of the turf were regular visitors, among them Fred Archer, George Fordham and Tom Cannon.

The premises were extensively renovated in the early 1960s.

LOWER WILLINGDON

BRITISH QUEEN: This was a blacksmith's forge until 1875 when the smith, William Denman sold it to Willingdon innkeeper Philip Measey for £46. In the First World War the Royal Naval Air Service, Dover Command, set up an airfield on land now covered by the houses of Coppice Avenue, Broad Street and Wannock Lane. Its entrance and hangars were near the pub and the crews of the airships that patrolled the Channel from there became regular customers. On the night of 22nd December 1915 one of the airships was recalled and, mistaking the lights of another airship for the field landing lights, crashed on top of it. Both burst into flames and their crews were killed.

The pub was sold to the Star Brewery in 1946 and the old house was demolished and the present premises built to the design of the brewery's architect, Herbert Compton.

MARESFIELD

CHEQUERS: There was a genuine German beer garden at the side of this hotel, facing the church, set up by a rich German who was living in the village. But he chose a bad time to open. The late summer of 1914 was not the right moment and his venture was not a success. Today all that remains of it are some massive gateposts which were built of stone from some ancient pig pounds in the village. The story of the beer garden is told by Thurston Hopkins in his *Old English Mills and Inns* (1927). He also gives an explanation for the strange looking tree on the inn sign bearing fruit not unlike grapes. He was apparently told by the landlord that it was a Service tree which was rarely found in England but there just happened to be one in the inn's garden. And the 'chequer tree' was, he was told, the old Sussex name for *Pyrus domesticus* or Service tree, known in the USA as the shadbush.

There are no trees in the Chequers' garden now – the last one went in the great storm of 16th October 1987 and that was a conifer. The licensee was inquiring of local nurseries in the spring of 1988 for another *Pyrus domesticus*.

MAYFIELD

The brewing of beer had disastrous results in this village in 1590. The parish records say it all: 'Upon Thursday, July 9, a great part of Maighfield was burned with fire. The fire first took hold of John Luck, his house, by chance of brewing, then it took the houses of William Cotin, Robert Wimble, an almshouse, Mr Neville, his barn and some other outhouses'.

81

MIDDLE HOUSE HOTEL: This fine, half timbered house bears the date 1575 so it obviously survived the fire. It was owned by Thomas Houghton, principal of Cliffords Inn, one of the Inns of Court in London, around 1614 and bought by the Baker family in 1669. A member of this family, the Rev Peter Baker, was vicar of Mayfield in 1728. Other owners include Edward Tench who bought it in 1841 and Alfred Tylor who bought it from him. There is a sliding panel between two of the attic rooms and it is said that one of the house's previous owners – he is not named – imprisoned his disobedient wife in one of the rooms and took food up to her himself and passed it through the panel. One day the poor wife discovered how to open the panel from her side and she climbed through it, dinner tray in hand, and lay in wait for her husband at the top of the stairs. When he climbed up with her next meal she hit him on the head with her tray!

In the 1920s the licence of the Old Star Inn was transferred to the Middle House. In the 1960s band leader Jack Payne and his wife Peggy Cochrane were the licensees and there were some merry impromptu concerts there after closing time.

NEWHAVEN

BRIDGE HOTEL: In 1623 this was the New Inn and remained so for 150 years until a drawbridge was built to replace the ferry crossing of the Ouse. This drawbridge was operated by five men – it took their combined strength to crank it open for tall masted ships to pass through – and they also had to collect tolls from people crossing from bank to bank of the river.

In premises overlooking the drawbridge Thomas Tipper brewed his famous ales which he supplied regularly to King George IV at the Royal Pavilion, Brighton. The remains of the brewery are now part of the hotel. The archway through which the waggons loaded with barrels creaked has been incorporated into the structure and the old Tipper Ale Office is part of the saloon bar. An adjoining bar parlour used to be reserved for the use of ships' captains of all nationalities, where they could talk of winds, and tides, currents and cargoes, and read the *Shipping Gazette*. Thomas Tipper, who died in 1785, contributed quite lavishly to the construction costs of the drawbridge and there is a carving of it on his tombstone in St Michael's churchyard.

The Bridge had some royal visitors in 1848. When the mob rose in Paris and forced the abdication of Louis Phillipe he and his queen fled to Normandy. There he discarded his fine clothes and his wig, and dressed in an old cloak and hat borrowed from a farmer, crossed with the queen, as Mr and Mrs Smith, in the steam packet *Express* to Newhaven. They were met by a local resident, Mr Sims, who had somehow received word of their coming, and escorted to the Bridge Hotel where they were greeted by Mrs Smith, the landlady.

While there the ex-king gave an interview to the editor of the *Sussex Weekly Advertiser*, Mr W Lee, and also received a private message from Queen Victoria who later arranged for a special train to take the refugees to London.

Over the door of the bedroom used by the royal Mr and Mrs Smith is a brass tablet bearing the Royal Arms. The *News Chronicle* of 13th June 1918 reported that it was given to the real Mrs Smith by Queen Victoria.

WHITE HART: An incident of horror worthy of Alfred Hitchcock occurred here in 1787 according to the *Sussex Weekly Advertiser*. One of the landlord's children had been put to bed when it started to cry. A maid found that a jackdaw 'which had been brought up tame in the house, had stolen into the bedroom and was pecking at the infant's eyes but providentially had not hurt them'.

A year later the same paper announced that the annual venison feast: 'is appointed to be held at the house of Thomas Kemp, the White Hart, Newhaven on Monday July 21. Dinner on the table at 2 o'clock.'

And a year after that there was a public sale of salvaged cargo at the house of Mr Kemp. It came from the *Syren* (master Thomas Hayman) which had crossed the Atlantic from Jamaica and had stranded near Beachy Head. Her cargo included 30 puncheons and some tillages of choice rum, which would be subject to Custom House duty of 5d and excise duty of 3s 7d a gallon.

When the road was widened in 1922 the White Hart was set further back. Subsequent road alterations have now left it in a pedestrian precinct.

NEWICK

BULL INN: This old inn was built in 1510 as a place of rest and refreshment for the pilgrims journeying between the cathedrals and shrines of Winchester, Chichester and

Canterbury. In those days its sign did not show the animal but a rolled sheet of parchment to indicate a papal bull or edict. The name, and in consequence the sign, was changed a number of times. When Daniel Gilbert bequeathed it to his wife Hannah in his will of 1867 he describes the property as 'the messuage called the Bull Inn; otherwise the Hatch; otherwise the Crown; otherwise the Bull and Butcher Inn with the butcher's shop adjoining'.

ROYAL OAK: The house and garden here was occupied by a maiden lady in 1851 and it was licensed as an alehouse in 1890 and did not get a full on licence until after the Second World War. Homemade fireworks called Newick Rousers were fairly lethal weapons in the hands of the more lively members of the Newick Bonfire Society. One was set off outside the Royal Oak and landed in the grocer's shop across the Green and set the curtains on fire. That was in 1914 – the year the society closed down. It was, however, revived after the Second World War.

NORMAN'S BAY

STAR INN: Originally the sluice house for the men working on the artificial waterway, Wallers Haven, in the 16th century. The sluice was designed by Stephen Waller of Hooe for the Commissioners of the Pevensey Levels and the house is referred to in a document of 1597 commenting on the 'infrequent passage of boats bringing iron from the Weald'. Hastings was the licensing authority for inns and alehouses in the Liberties so the Sluice had to apply to Hastings magistrates until the procedure was changed by the Justices of the Peace Bill of 1949. William Piddlesden was selling beer from the Sluice House in 1596 without a licence and after he had been trading for a fortnight he was caught and committed to jail until he could find a respectable citizen to guarantee his good behaviour.

The inn's name was changed to the Star in 1801 by Henry Lingham who had married a Miss Elizabeth Starr.

This was one of the busiest spots for the smuggling trade. It acted as a distribution point and tracks from the Sluice led to the Lamb on the marshes, the Red Lion at Hooe and west to safe houses near Pevensey. In 1833 it was the scene of a fierce fight between the coastguards and the smugglers. The coastguards were victorious and three smugglers were killed, five captured and later transported and all the contraband seized.

NORTHIAM

SIX BELLS: In 1762 wheelwright William Wilmhurst bequeathed this property to his wife, May. On her death it was to be divided between his brothers, Stephen, an innkeeper of Cranbrook and Thomas who was a staymaker. It was called the Six Bells then and the name has never been changed. In a deed of 1779 a brewhouse, cellars, stables and woodhouses belonged to the property which a year later was sold to a victualler, Thomas Smith, for £400.

A few years later the Honourable John Byng, that inveterate rider around Sussex in the 18th century, dropped in. 'A village of cleanliness and beauty mixed with shade' he wrote of Northiam in his diary. 'The landlord, after putting my horse into a good stable, carried me into his family dinner and I readily sat down with him, his wife, two children and a young man to a boiled leg of mutton, turnips and apple pie.'

OFFHAM

CHALKPIT INN: The first railway in Sussex ran from here in 1809. It carried the chalk from the Offham Hill quarry through two tunnels under the A275 road with a 400 feet long inclined plane to the Papermill Cut where it could be transferred to barges and taken away. A loaded wagon carrying 1½ tons could descend in 1½ minutes drawing an empty one up as it went down.

The tunnels are still there today but the cut has gone and the Ouse is no longer navigable above Lewes for anything but the smallest of boats. The railway closed in the 1870s, its work done.

OLD HEATHFIELD

STAR INN: This inn started its life as an alehouse for the stone-masons building the church that occupied the site of the present church of All Saints. In the 15th century Wasseline Maydlow, described as an innkeeper and stonemason, ran the house and he was succeeded by his widow, Elinor. It continued in the same family until 1476 when a carpenter, John Woollvene turns up in the early records as keeper of the 'Starre at Church'.

In 1606 Robert Hunt, the vicar of Heathfield sailed away for the New World with several regulars of the Star Inn. At the age of 37 he had been chosen by the Archbishop of Canterbury as 'an honest, religious and courageous divine' to accompany Richard Hakluyt on his expedition to discover new lands across the sea. He was the first clergyman to settle in America and there is a plaque to his memory in the pub. It was given by the American and British Commonwealth Association of the United States in 1957 to mark the 350th anniversary of the founding of the State of Virginia and commemorates: 'Robert Hunt, vicar of Heathfield, and chaplain to the expedition which founded the first permanent English settlement in North America at Jamestown, Virginia, in 1607'.

The Star has a list of all its licensees since its early alehouse days. It also has on one of its walls a chart of the Bay of Biscay and surrounding seas, which appears to be of mid 18th century origin, and was once the property of a Captain Adams. No one knows quite why it is there.

ORE

HARE AND HOUNDS: There was a small stone alehouse with a theatre attached to it on this site until Boxing Day, 1867. On that day fire destroyed the boards on which Edmund Kean had walked.

How one of the top tragedians of the 19th century came to give his Shylock before an appreciative audience of Hastings' residents is told in the *Sussex Weekly Advertiser* of October 1821. It appeared that Kean was on holiday at Hastings, which had no theatre of its own, and was walking near Fairlight one day when he met a young man from the company at the Hare and Hounds theatre. This young man had a sad tale to tell. The actors had not been paid because a wild beast show had proved too strong a rival attraction and the management was broke. Even the scenic artist, T Sidney Cooper, had lost a £5 note and his watch.

Kean agreed to come to the rescue of his fellow Thespians. Handbills were quickly printed announcing his appearance as Shylock in the *Merchant of Venice* 'for one night only'. When this news reached the ears of R W Elliston, who had taken Drury Lane for a season and planned to open with Kean as

Richard III, he rushed down to Hastings to see what his star was up to. He ended up on the Hare and Hounds boards himself, appearing in his own play, *The Liar*.

The box office takings from that one night in 1821 was enough to get the company out of its financial trouble – but only for a time. Shortly afterwards it closed for good.

The Hare and Hounds today bears no resemblance to the little inn sketched by Francis Grose on a visit to the area in 1790. But its theatrical connections are still remembered. There is a plaque commemorating the old theatre on the side of the inn where it stood. It was unveiled by Sir Herbert Beerbohm Tree in 1914.

PEACEHAVEN

SUSSEX COASTER: Pubs do not usually have teapots on their roofs but this one does. There on the gable ridge sits a jumbo-sized teapot, with a bit missing from just behind the spout to reveal its concrete filling.

It has been there since the premises were built in the 1920s by builders, Bacon Brothers. It was put in position during the topping out ceremony by William Kenney, possibly because the new building was to be run as a tea room.

It is only in recent years that it has become a pub. After being a tea room it was a club, then, when first licensed it was called the Gay Highlander, later changed to the Sussex Coaster. When it was re-roofed in the early 1980s the tea pot was removed and replaced.

PILTDOWN

PILTDOWN MAN: The gravel pits of Piltdown were a happy hunting ground, just before the First World War, for solicitor and amateur geologist Charles Dawson and a young Jesuit, Teilhard de Chardin, who was also fascinated by fossils. At the end of a day's searching through the spoils from the quarrying operations at the pits they may well have dropped into the village pub, the Lamb, for a drink.

And no doubt the regulars at the Lamb raised their glasses and drank to Piltdown Man when, in 1916, it was announced to the academic world, that the missing link between man and ape had been found. Darwin's theory of evolution had been vindicated by the discovery of *Eaonthropus dawsonii* – the name given to the early man whose skull and jawbone had been discovered in the gravel.

Piltdown Man was an accepted link in the human chain for some 40 years. The Lamb's name was changed in his honour in 1949 but four years later came a nasty shock – Piltdown Man was a forgery. Fluorine tests had shown that the jaw bone was that of an orang utang, the skull of a modernish man and the associated remains specimens from a museum collection. The site had been salted – but by whom?

The next excitement was to name the villain. Was it Dawson, the respected local solicitor? De Chardin, the priest? Sir Arthur Smith Woodward, keeper of palaeontology at the British Museum? Today, more than 70 years later, the hoaxer has not been unmasked for certain – and the Piltdown Man is still an inn, if not a fossil remain.

PLUMPTON GREEN

PLOUGH INN: The old Plough Inn was a casualty of the Second World War. It was then in Beresford Lane and was demolished to make way for a grass airfield to be used as an emergency landing ground for the Spitfires and Hurricanes fighting the Battle of Britain.

The ground was fairly marshy so the Air Ministry had to build a fairly elaborate system of drains so the aircraft did not get bogged down when they landed. After the war these drains proved a safe haven for the local foxes when the hunt was up.

The present Plough is a post-war building.

POLEGATE

HORSE AND GROOM: Shortly after the Lewes–Polegate–Eastbourne turnpike road was built in 1819 an alehouse opened just behind the toll house where travellers had to stop and pay to pass on. Many of them would drop in for a drink before continuing their journey to the delight and financial profit of innkeeper William Bodle who was there from 1850 to 1858 when William Humphrey succeeded him and stayed until 1866. After him came Thomas Vine who went into partnership with a Mr Hemsley in 1870.

In 1882 Alexander Hurst bought the inn. With his partner, Cardwell, he already had the Junction Hotel and the concession for the refreshment room at Polegate Station. A few years later these two formed the Star Brewery Company with its headquarters in Eastbourne.

In the 1930s the Horse and Groom was rebuilt to the design of brewery architect Herbert Compton who was much given to beams and plaster. To emphasise the name he incorporated a couple of panels in the south elevation showing in each a horse and groom, believed to be derived from a painting by the famous painter of horses and sporting scenes, J F Herring Senior (1795–1865).

RINGMER

COCK INN: No barnyard fowl is commemorated by this inn's name but the 'cock' or lead horse that would be added to a team when a particularly steep hill had to be climbed. Coachmen used to hire extra horses here in preparation for the uphill slog to Tunbridge Wells. It has been a licensed house since the time of the Commonwealth and in earlier days the four rooms on the ground floor were licensed separately and identified by numbers on porcelain plates. Two such plates survive.

ANCHOR: The discovery of a basket with an umbrella neatly placed across it on the bank of the pond near the vicarage resulted in a trial of four men for multiple rape and murder in 1838. The body of Hannah Smith, a tinker from Lewes, was recovered from the pond and buried next day in the churchyard. An inquest at the Anchor heard that she had had drinks there and at the Green Man with another tinker 'General' Washer and that they met up with some young men. Hannah left the Anchor with the young men at 11pm and was not seen alive again.

At first Washer was suspected of her murder but Police Superintendent Francis Fagain received some anonymous letters which lead him to arrest Charles Briggs, John Pockney and Stephen Stedman as well.

In the report of the trial in the *Sussex Express* Pockney claimed that Hannah had agreed to have sex with all of them: 'I took her into the fields and had connexion with her' he is quoted as saying. 'Briggs went next, and Stedman next, I went a second time, I had her work box, Stedman had a snuff box and some other articles.'

The judge, Lord Alderson, suggested to the jury that Hannah had fallen into the pond in a drunken stupor. Briggs was discharged. Pockney got two years for larceny and Stedman 18 months.

In the 18th century the inn was called the Blue Anchor and here in April 1797 Verrall and Son offered for sale by auction 36 pairs of 'exceeding good unwhitened sheets manufactured by the poor of Ringmer parish' as well as the effects of Mr John Davey.

A quart mug inscribed 'Anchor Inn Ringmer' is in the Barbican House Museum in Lewes. It is made of Mocha ware, which is decorated with fern-like markings to resemble the mocha stone or moss agate. It was first produced in England in the 1780s mainly for taverns and general domestic use.

The inn is the headquarters of the Ringmer Cricket Club and had records and pictures going back to the early 18th century as well as a strange looking bat which was used in a match between two teams of 'clowns' at Lewes Priory Cricket Club in the 1870s.

ROBERTSBRIDGE

SEVEN STARS: This medieval timber-framed building was a private house until the early 18th century and at one time belonged to the Abbey of Robertsbridge.

The Cistercian order of monks at the Abbey received a charter from Richard I in 1198, four years after the Abbot of Robertsbridge had helped negotiate his release from imprisonment in Bavaria by Henry VI, Emperor of Germany. Local legend has it that the ransom for the king was paid here – but it was not. The Abbot of Robertsbridge and the Abbot of the nearby Boxley Abbey had travelled to Bavaria in 1193 and when Richard was arraigned before the Council of Empire at Worms in the Rhine Valley, accused of procuring assassins to kill the Marquis of Montferrat, a rival king of Jerusalem, they were there. Richard was acquitted but the Emperor demanded a ransom of 150,000 marks before he would release him. The cash was put into his hands 14 months later and Richard landed back in England in 1194. What may have given rise to the legend is that the ransom was so heavy that every man in England had to give up a quarter of his income. Everything had to be sold and turned into money, including church plate and property. Perhaps the two abbots were the appointed receivers of contributions from this part of the county, which they then passed on to the central ransom fund. Not that they could have done this on the premises – the house was not built until 200 or so years later.

OSTRICH: This inn opposite the railway station was built around 1855 and acquired its unusual name from the coat of arms of the Allfrey family who were Lords of the Manor from 1822. On the Allfrey shield are the heads of three ostriches with crowns around their necks.

ROTHERFIELD

KINGS ARMS: A former tithe barn which was later used as a bakery and became an inn in the early 18th century. The Court Rolla and old rate books give details of some of the previous tenants. In 1724, for instance, Adam Farmer was in occupation paying a yearly rental of 10d – and for that he got the stables, gardens and 'other appointments' as well.

In 1953 the licensee was the famous cricketer Maurice Tate who, during his career, took 2,211 wickets for Sussex. His father, Fred Tate, had been an innkeeper – his last house was the Burrell Arms at Haywards Heath – so not surprisingly Maurice went into the business when he retired from first class cricket. He did not desert the game totally. When he was at the Kings Arms and later, when he moved to the Greyhound at Wadhurst, he was coaching at Tonbridge School and busy umpiring.

An incident took place in the tap room around the time of the First World War that left three regulars looking most uncomfortable. One of them was Jim Briggs who had been told firmly by his wife that morning that he must come straight home from work for his dinner at midday. But he did not turn up on time for the meat pudding and three veg she had ready at the appointed time. She gave him some 15 minutes grace then put the food in a basket with a knife and fork and marched into the tap room. Briggs and two friends were sitting there with their pints of ale. Mrs Briggs said not a word but spread a cloth on a table next to them, spread out her dinner and proceeded to eat it. When she had finished she packed up her basket and left. Briggs was never late home again.

CATT'S INN: This was an inn from 1635 and then a grocer's and draper's shop. It had reverted to its original purpose by 1769 when a vestry meeting was held there for the paying of the annual accounts. It probably got its name from a tenant bearing the name of Catt which was quite common in the locality. There was a Thomas Catt at the Swan in Rotherfield in 1747, and a Mrs Catt, innholder, was buried in 1751. In the Rates Book of 1741 Francis Hutchinson was assessed for the 'Catt House'.

In March 1809 the inn was described as 'house and premises, late Cat Inn' and later it was locally known as the Three Cats because there were three cats on the inn sign.

ROTTINGDEAN

WHITE HORSE INN: The original 16th century house was demolished in 1934 when the present building was put up. In the old days it was a busy coaching inn and one night the Brighton to Eastbourne coach left the shelter of its courtyard – and disappeared. It was found the next day at the foot of the cliffs at Saltdean. It had been blown over by the strong winds, and passengers and horses were all dead.

The inn offered stabling for 40 horses and in 1820 Crossweller and Attree started a new coach, the Royal Charlotte, which could do the Brighton to Dover run in 10 hours. In the same year the Union line ran a coach the 114 miles to Margate via Rottingdean.

The White Horse was also frequently used as an auction house. The cargo and remains of a ship wrecked off the coast was sold here and, in 1813, so was Rottingdean windmill. This mill had for many years been used by the local smugglers to signal, by the setting of its sails, when it was safe for ships at sea to land their cargo. This job was often done by the vicar, the Rev Dr Hooker, who was in spiritual charge of the parish between 1792 and 1838.

A later licensee, Stephen Welfare, continued the transport tradition of the inn in the late 19th century by running a horse bus to carry mail and passengers to Brighton. This vehicle could only seat six and it was advisable to book in advance. It was so uncomfortable and cramped that it was known locally as the coffin on wheels.

RUSHLAKE GREEN

HORSE AND GROOM: According to an old Land Tax map this inn was owned by the Widow Pankhurst in 1810. By 1841 it was being run by Trayton Burgess and cricketer James Hoadley took over in 1887 and 'batted well and scored 20 runs' in a village cricket match.

A later landlord made the mistake of displaying one of the skulls from Warbleton Priory in the bar. He thought that it would attract customers but all it did was turn his beer sour so he passed it on to a neighbouring farmer. There are two skulls in Warbleton Priory and there are a lot of strange stories connected with them. Stephen Ziegler, whose grandparents moved to the Priory in 1906, gives the details in his book *Warbleton Priory* (1977). The origin of the skulls is doubtful but the curses attached to them are specific.

If a stranger should look at them for any length of time there would be a terrible storm.

If anyone should touch them he or she would pass through the valley of the shadow of death.

If they are buried or removed from the Priory every animal there will die.

These curses all reportedly came true. Animals died, whirlwinds occurred if anyone reached for a spade, and people suffered from mysterious diseases. The skulls disappeared around the turn of the century but one turned up in a Brighton antique shop, where it caused all sorts of chaos. It was advertised for sale in the *Times* and went back to the Priory. It was joined by the other skull, packed in a biscuit tin, and now both are happily at home.

Before there was a skull at the pub, the Warbleton Friendly Society used to meet there. On 26th May 1866, a procession left the pub, led by Eastbourne Saxhorn Band and an officer carrying a Union Jack, to mark the society's foundation day.

Rye

The mayor and jurats who ran this ancient Cinque Port laid down particular conditions when they granted licences to alehouses. On 22nd September 1571, Nicholas Fowler was licensed to keep an alehouse for one year. He must at all times: 'Have it furnished with convenient victuals for the relief of his poor neighbours and other honest wayfaring or travelling persons, not omitting to supply fish on fish days.' He was not to: 'Maintain any beds, suffer any unlawful games, nor sell any victuals in time of divine service.' He had to close at 9pm in summer and 8pm in winter.

MERMAID: The French burned down the medieval wattle and daub alehouse in 1377 during one of their raids on Rye. It was rebuilt in 1420 and in 1636 was owned by Thomas Peacock who built and endowed Rye Grammar School. He partly paid for the headmaster's salary by an annuity of £4 secured on the Mermaid and this was redeemed for £50 some years later. The Mermaid entered into a turbulent phase of its history in the 18th century when the Hawkhurst Gang, founded by George Gray, virtually adopted it as their head-quarters. They would plan and prepare for their smuggling forays here and celebrate their success 'carousing and smoking their pipes with their loaded pistols on the table before them' according to a contemporary account.

The gang became so powerful that no one dared inform against them and no magistrate dared convict should one of them be brought to court. On one occasion Thomas Moore, a smuggler who had been quickly bailed when brought to court, stormed into the Mermaid, where the bailiff who had informed on him, was quietly drinking. Moore grabbed the man and pulled him down the street to the harbour and was about to throw him in to the water when the captain of a revenue sloop moored there came to the bailiff's rescue.

The Mermaid's reputation as a safe house for the free-traders perhaps accounts for the fact that it was rarely used for civic functions after around 1750. In earlier days it had shared these occasions, such as the annual mayor making ceremony and dinners for the barons of the Cinque Ports with the George. Changes in the laws of the land and social patterns brought the smuggling era to an end and the inn's business declined along with its reputation. By 1913 it was being run as a club by Mrs May Aldington, the mother of novelist Richard Aldington. It did not reopen as an hotel until 1945.

In spite, or perhaps because of its chequered history, it has had some important visitors. Queen Elizabeth I may have stayed there on her visit to Rye in 1573 although local tradition says she slept at the Customs House, then known as Grene Hall. The French Ambassador definitely dropped in on his way to London in 1654 and later visitors have been actress Ellen Terry, American novelist Henry James before he bought Lamb House, Hilaire Belloc, Rupert Brooke, Ford Maddox Ford and, of course, Russell Thorndyke who used the inn as the background for his series of Dr Syn books about smuggling on Romney Marshes.

G EORGE HOTEL: This inn was moved from the Butchery opposite the town hall to the High Street around 1740 and in 1818 Lewes Meryon added a fine assembly room which was popular with the farmers from the outlying districts when they came into town for the cattle market. It was also used by the Corporation of Rye for various civic occasions involving food. When the Lord Mayor of London, Thomas Farncomb, came to open the railway at Rye in 1850, the George provided a sumptuous banquet. The chandeliers in the assembly room were lit by gas for the first time and glittered upon a stately company which consumed a first course of salmon, turbot, sole and other seafood; a second course of capons with mushroom sauce, turkeys with truffle sauce, tongue and creamed spinach, legs of mutton, sirloin of beef, pigeon pies, chickens and veal. The third course was of ducklings, pea fowl and goslings; the fourth puddings, tarts, cremes and Charlotte Russe and for dessert there were assorted fruits, cakes and nuts. Refreshments of a more modest kind were provided when a jury was impanelled 'to sit on ye body of a black person found in a well in Mr Hovenden's fields'. The account read: 'To wine 4s; to beer for the men that found him 1s 4d.'

There was an odd little ceremony in 1738 when the licensee was Michael Woollett. The accounts record that '£2 spent in drinking the King's health being the Queen's birthday'. It was in 1719, when Queen Anne came to the throne, that the George opened in the High Street after its move from the Butchery. Any excuse for a party, as they say.

The annual mayor-making ceremony involves, for some reason, the throwing of hot pennies into the street where they are scrabbled for by the local children. This quaint custom takes place from the balcony of the George to this day.

ST LEONARDS

BO-PEEP HOTEL: The nursery rhyme about Little Bo Peep who had lost her sheep dates from the days of Elizabeth I, long long before these premises were built. The local reason given for the strange name is that bo-peep was a game of hide and seek and that is what the smugglers used to play with the Revenue men in this area in the 1800s. It was first licensed by Robert Dunk in 1810 and called the New England Bank but two years later Richard Ockenden took over and renamed the inn. During his occupancy – in 1817 – one of England's most famous lyric poets, John Keats, is said to have stayed there. The old inn was demolished when the

West Marina railway station was built in the 1850s. The present building is Victorian.

WELCOME STRANGER: A former licensee, Mrs Price, was the model for Val Prinseps famous painting *The Goose Girl* which hung in the Royal Academy in 1900 and was sold from there to the Walker Art Gallery Liverpool. The background of the painting shows Pevensey Castle and Westham Church and Mrs Price, then Miss Laura Gell, was the daughter of the landlord of the Castle Inn at Pevensey Bay. Mr Gell, who often took the artist out fishing, was also used as a model for a number of his paintings.

WARRIORS GATE: Limeburner George Hyland bought the land on which his kilns stood in 1832 and built a public house 'by the name and sign of the Warrior's Gate' on it. But for several years after it opened people called it the Warhouse Gate as it stood on a field belonging to Germany Farm and known as Warhouse Field. It is now the London Road.

BULL INN: This has been an inn since 1736 when it was bought by James Kenward from Rye brewer Alfred Dunk. In the documents of that transaction it is described as 'commonly known as St Mary's' because it was close to the church of that name. All that remains of the old church is a wall of the churchyard where, it is said, many of the Dutch crew from the *Amsterdam* were buried. This ship, an East Indiaman bound for Batavia, broke her rudder in Pevensey Bay and then came ashore off Bulverhythe at 3 o'clock on a Sunday afternoon in January 1748 'with firing a great many guns'.

There were three women aboard and about 40 sick men. Mr George Worge said in a letter to Mr John Collier on 17th January 1748: 'The value of the ship and cargo is uncertain but £200,000 was the general estimate. There were three women on board who are now at Hastings. When I was down there were about 40 sick men in the ship which they afterwards got out and sent to Hastings. I saw Sir Chs Eversfield there, who told me he was down when she came on shore and that all the crew were drunk, and so were all of them that I saw yesterday'.

Nearly all the 28 chests of silver the *Amsterdam* was carrying were brought ashore in spite of the efforts of looters and wreckers to beat the Customs men to it. Some 220 years later, when the sea scoured under the old defences and encroached inland the *Amsterdam*, or what was left of her, was brought to light again. Since then work on the wreck has resulted in the recovery of much that was thought lost and is now on show at the Hastings Museum and the new shipwreck Heritage Centre at Rock-a-Nore.

SEAFORD

Records stored in the Town Chest of the Cinque Port of Seaford disclose that in 1642 'the selling of ale without a licence was carried to such lengths that two persons were fined 20s or be whipped'.

LORD ADMIRAL: Formerly the Bay Hotel and before that a private house and some cottages which Thomas Crook pulled down in 1869 when he built his new hotel with a coach house and stabling extending as far as West Lane. Later on these stables were replaced by an extension to the hotel adding a dining room, billiards room and public bar.

Romance blossomed on the premises in 1882 – and it all started on Valentine's Day when the steamship *Gannet* bound for London from Calcutta with a cargo of tea, coffee, cotton, grain and spices, was wrecked in Seaford Bay. Her crew was brought safely ashore by breeches-buoy and one of the officers had the ship's papers with him. They got soaked with the sea water and a young chambermaid at the hotel helped him dry them out. They fell in love, married, and he took her out to India with him on his next voyage.

WELLINGTON: A newspaper report of a mystery visitor to this inn in October 1845 caused its name to be changed from the New Inn to the Wellington. The *Sussex Express*, the only newspaper to carry the story, hinted heavily that the visitor was the Duke of Wellington, victor of Waterloo and now Chief of the Armed Forces. He was there, said the paper, perhaps to assess the potential of Seaford Bay as a safe anchorage in times of conflict. One of the founders of Seaford Museum of Local History, Mrs Joan Astell, took the trouble to check the Wellesley family archives at Stratfield Saye in 1974 and found nothing to indicate that the Duke had visited Seaford then, or at any other time.

But 100 years earlier the newspaper report was believed and when the inn changed hands in the 1880s its name was changed and on show was the 'Duke's Room'.

To mark Queen Victoria's golden jubilee a drinking fountain was put up outside the inn, on the site of the old King's well, but it had to be moved fairly soon to the Salts as it proved too much of a traffic hazard, even in those days.

HOLE-IN-THE-WALL: In the 18th century this was the Duke of Cumberland's Head or more usually known as the Duke's Head. In April 1761 an announcement in the *Sussex Weekly Advertiser* informed readers that 'a four wheel chaise and four able horses are to be let to any part of England from the Duke's Head at Seaford.'

In those days the innkeeper, or master, was Israel Midhurst who died in February 1771 'of a fit'. His widow carried on the business and she was in charge when the Seaford Amicable Society met there and when the Wealdish Ripiers devoured for their breakfast 'four stone of good whitings, one 6d loaf, two pounds of butter, three quarts of strong beer and five and a half quarters of geneva and then quitted the coast tolerably satisfied'. Ripiers were the mobile fishmongers of the day, collecting the catch as it was landed and taking the fish inland to sell.

By June 1792 the inn's name had been changed to the Pelham Arms and in the *Sussex Weekly Advertiser* appeared this announcement: 'A diligence sets out at 6 o'clock in the morning every Sunday, Tuesday, Thursday and Saturday and arrives at the London Coach office, Lewes, in time for the London coach and waits for the return of the London coach. From Seaford to Lewes 3s 6d per passenger. From Newhaven to Lewes 2s 6d.'

In the early 1950s the Pelham Arms was closed for re-decoration and refurbishment. When it re-opened it bore the name it has today.

THE BUCKLE: The inn that bears this name today was built in 1964 at a cost of some £28,000 beside the Old Buckle which has been demolished. The old inn was formerly a couple of farm cottages and became a beerhouse around 1830, shortly after the Duke of Wellington's Beer Act. It was run by the Venus family for many years.

Tom Venus had it in 1900 and he was still there in 1949 when the *Evening News* reported that he had to keep an eye on the sea to check whether or not he was going to get any customers. When the tide was high and it was blowing strongly from the south-west the road past the Buckle was impassable. Flying spray would blind motorists and the crashing waves would sweep the shingle over the road to the danger of cars and drivers. 'Road closed' signs would be put up and traffic diverted and Tom would know it would not be worth opening up. In that same newspaper report he also disclosed that the Buckle's windows were never opened or cleaned in all the years he had been there. 'What's the use,' he said. 'The sea would have salted them up straight away'.

When the new inn was planned in 1963 there was talk of calling it the Goldfish after the Goldfish Club, whose members were RAF aircrew who had been saved from the sea. But local feeling proved too strong. It had always been the Buckle and the locals did not want the name to be changed.

SEDLESCOMBE

QUEENS HEAD: There has been an inn on the village green since 1523 – a gabled house with a large cross-shaped chimney stack and a wide fireplace with seats beside it. The sign of the Queens Head went up to mark Queen Elizabeth I's journey through Sussex to Rye where she was lavishly entertained by the mayor and jurats in 1573.

In the 18th century some five or six farmers met here and drew up a document, which they all signed, promising to support each other against the blackmailing demands of the local smugglers – no doubt the notorious Hawkhurst gang. In 1841 James Breeds was the owner and the innkeeper was Stephen Turner but soon afterwards the inn was sold to a brewery.

It was in 1886 that the Sedlescombe Men's Friendly Society was formed and it took over the organisation of the May Day holiday celebrations previously run by the church. For the occasion huge puddings were boiled in the coppers in the Queens Head kitchen by Mrs Nightingale, the wife of the innkeeper John Nightingale.

TICEHURST

It was customary for the parish bills to be paid once a year at one of three inns in the village and for the annual parish dinner to be held in another inn – so spreading the benefit of parochial gathering evenly between the local licensed houses. In 1792 the accounts were paid at the Chequers and the parish allowances spent on a meal at the Bell. In 1795 the dinner was at the Duke of York and in 1799 the innkeeper was paid £1 13s 6d for the refreshments he supplied after a confirmation service. There was a tithe feast at the Bell in 1793 and the bill for the drink was £4 17s 5d. Some 19 stone of beef was consumed and it cost 3s 4d a stone.

BELL INN: The Faythfule or Faithfull family ran this inn in the 15th century, according to the history which present licensee Mrs Pamela Tate has had researched. A list of all the licensees from those early days is framed in the saloon bar.

Mrs Tate, whose mother Elizabeth Reeve ran the pub from 1953 to 1970, has a fine collection of bells including one dating from the coronation of Queen Victoria.

UCKFIELD

MAIDEN'S HEAD: The name, according to Sussex historian Mark Anthony Lower, refers to the Virgin Mary. Locally it is said that it used to be called the King's Head and its name was changed by order of Elizabeth I. There was a King's Head inn, almost opposite, where Victorian diarist Augustus Hare, once stayed. It later became the Uckfield United Services Club.

The Maiden's Head was a coaching inn when Church Street was the main road going via Hempstead Lane to Framfield to join the Eastbourne to London road, now the A22. The petty sessions were held there until a consortium of magistrates and business men decided that alternative premises were needed. They formed the Uckfield Public Hall Company and in 1877 built themselves a courtroom and meeting house with seating for 300 people. It flourished financially as local organisations were only too pleased to hire it for their functions and it was eventually bought by East Sussex County Council and continued as a magistrates court.

In the Uckfield Visitors' Guide of 1869 the inn is advertised by Richard Cloake as a 'commercial and family hotel and posting house' with 'carriages to and from the station which will await the arrival of every train.'

Horses and carriages 'of all descriptions' were still being advertised some 20 years later when the proprietress was H Barnes.

ALMA ARMS: The Allied Forces – those of Great Britain, France, Sardinia and Turkey – had a famous victory over the Russians at the Battle of Alma River in the Crimea in 1854, the year this pub was built. The present licensee, Sam Hughes, is the third generation of the same family to run it. Robert Kelvin Griffin was succeeded by his daughter, who married Bob Turner and they were succeeded by their daughter Joy, who married Sam. Between 1927 and 1937 the pub was the headquarters of the Uckfield Volunteer Fire Brigade and its two appliances were housed in a shed at the back.

UDIMORE

KINGS HEAD: The churchwardens and members of the parochial church council 'in vestry assembled' were regular patrons here in the 18th century. They found their meetings thirsty work and the parish would pay for their drinks and the amount spent, such as £1 7s 6d on one occasion in 1774, faithfully recorded in the accounts. 'Parliamenteering' was more expensive. The amount of £3 7s 9d was spent in the same year at the Kings Head, then run by Mrs Brown, 'on the occasion of Mr Willson gaining his election as member for the county.'

The vicar of Udimore, Peter Simons, was presented before the Archdeaconry Court at Lewes on 6th December 1603 for 'baptising a catt'. He appeared and denied the charge and was ordered to turn up with four witnesses on 17th January in the church of St Andrew at Alfriston. After several adjournments the case was ordered to be heard in Rye on 28th March 1604 but there is no record of what happened to the rector, or what exactly he was doing to the 'catt'.

WADHURST

THE GREYHOUND: This posting inn dating back to the 16th century, was one of the Hawkhurst Gang's safe houses. In the 1950s Sussex cricketer Maurice Tate took it over. He moved here from the King's Arms at Rotherfield and before that he had been at the Nevill Crest and Gun at Eridge for a short time. He collapsed and died suddenly at the Greyhound in May 1956 and was buried in Wadhurst churchyard.

WARBLETON

WARBILL-IN-TUN: A handshake ended in tragedy in this old inn in 1910. A local farmer fell down the unguarded cellar steps, cracked his skull and died three weeks later in hospital at Eastbourne.

The fall, or the reason for it, was partly his own fault according to some of the evidence given at the inquest. The farmer, William Reeves of Chantry Farm had been drinking with friends at the pub at lunchtime and returned in the afternoon after doing some work on the farm.

At 7.30pm Robert Anderson, a bailiff from Wadhurst arrived with a friend. He and Reeves knew each other and, according to licensee Albert Wood, they talked together 'very quiet and comfortable'. After half an hour Anderson, who had had 'two wee drops of Scotch' got up to go and at the door turned to say goodnight. Reeves met him at the door and they left the bar together.

Warbleton chicken fattener George Avard, hinted heavily in his evidence that Anderson had pushed Reeves down the steps on purpose. 'I told him so and he got angry and said that he was a sportsman and 60 years old, and he would knock my head through the wall' he said.

Anderson insisted that he and Reeves were good friends and had never had a quarrel. As he went to shake hands Reeves squeezed his four fingers and as he turned his hand to free them, caught hold of his thumb. 'I said – you're going to break my thumb – and pushed him away with my left hand' he told the jury 'I then walked away. I did not know he had fallen down the cellar steps any more than the man in the moon'. Reeves was found in the cellar unconscious and bleeding from the back of the head. He was carried upstairs and taken home in a cart.

Verdict of the inquest jury was that death was due to misadventure and Anderson was exonerated from all blame. But the incident gave rise to some local tension, according to a relative of Reeves who called at the inn a couple of years ago. The village was divided in its opinion of the verdict and who was to blame but there was no suggestion that the unguarded cellar steps were a contributory factor.

The inn, which was called the Two Tuns in 1690, acquired its punning name much later. It has been much altered and the cellar steps have discreetly disappeared from public view.

WILLINGDON

RED LION: This village local, now almost totally surrounded by new houses, has surprisingly radical literary connections. George Orwell's political fable *Animal Farm*, first published in 1945, has several references to it. The farmer, Mr Jones, spent a lot of his time 'sitting in the taproom of the Red Lion at Willingdon, complaining to anyone who would listen, of the monstrous injustices he had suffered in being turned out of his own property by a pack of good-for-nothing animals'.

Eric Arthur Blair, who wrote as George Orwell was at school at St Cyprians, Eastbourne from 1911–1916. He hated the town but liked to walk on the Downs and visit the neighbouring villages. Willingdon in those days was quite unspoilt and the present Red Lion, which was built in 1907, was probably its most modern building.

It is the third pub of the same name on the site. The first was a little cottage alehouse approached through an iron gate and up a brick paved garden path. The second inn was a half timbered house and it had a mangle room attached where the local washerwomen could wring out their clothes at a cost of a penny a bundle.

WHEATSHEAF: Two cottages were converted to a beer-house in the 1850s and traded without incident until the Star Brewery, which then owned the house, decided it needed brightening up. Just before the First World War the tenancy was offered to Mr and Mrs Edward Cuthbert, rent free for the first year, so they could raise the standard. They were there for the next 40 years and were succeeded by their son-in-law William Yeoell who died tragically in 1955. The next licensee was George Skinner, former manager of Hastings United football team.

The pub's mock Tudor beamed facade is not original. The premises were given the 'olde worlde' treatment by Star Brewery architect Herbert Compton in 1934. And it was about this time that its beer only licence was changed to a full licence.

WINCHELSEA

NEW INN: That aristocratic 18th century traveller around Sussex, the Honourable John Byng has rather an odd entry in his diary in respect of his visit to this ancient port, now many miles from the sea. He writes: 'The New Inn I passed by, inquiring for the Bear, but the landlord said "This is the only inn for my Bear has run away". So I searched in haste for bedrooms and found two excellent ones and a good parlour'. Was it of the landlord of the New Inn that he tactlessly inquired about the Bear? Was there once an inn called the Bear in Winchelsea? Where exactly did his search for rooms lead him? Was it to the Castle Inn, now closed – or to the Bridge down on the Strand?

The New Inn has changed little since the Georgian days in which it was built. In 1837 it was left by innkeeper George Harrod to his wife and in 1899 Mrs Mary Kenward was running it as a family hotel. A wine merchant's brochure, found in the mid 1980s when some restoration work was being done, gives details of the wholesale costs of wines and spirits in the year 1800/01. Yates and Wood of Hythe in Kent quoted:

Port wine	£100–£110 a pipe
Madeira	£66–£76 a pipe
Sherry	£48–£52 " "
Rum	£16–£19 a gallon.
Foreign brandy	£21–£25
Hollands genever	£21–£25
British brandy	£14–£15 a gallon
British gin	£11–£15 a gallon
Cordials	£14–£17

Three months' credit of 2½ per cent discount for King's money.

A pipe is 105 gallons so the port works out at about £1 a gallon but rum seems surprisingly expensive at about £2 a bottle. Even British gin is more than a pound a bottle, taking it that the pre-metric bottle of spirits held about a pint. The wine list is clearly printed so there is no mistaking the quantities and cost.

WITHYHAM

DORSET ARMS: Isaac Rogers of Witheham was in trouble in October 1677 for keeping an illegal alehouse. The Quarter Sessions Records which report his case do not name the alehouse. Perhaps he was the first to launch this inn on its long history of providing rest and refreshment. Isaac paints a sorry picture of his life and admits 'total ignorance of the laws and statutes of the kingdom' as he most humbly begs the justices to mitigate the fine 'which for his offence he doth acknowledge himself worthy to suffer'.

He says 'being very sickly by nature' he only sold beer 'being much solicited by Justice Bakers Colliers' to do so 'and to keep himself, and family, from being a charge on the parish.' He promises not to do it again and he is supported by the rector, Isaac Burges, churchwardens William Morley and John Constable, and three parishioners, who say they would forever acknowledge themselves obliged if the Bench would look favourably on the petitioner.

The Dorset Arms is named in a survey of alehouses in 1781 and it was then owned by Hartfield victuallers Obadiah Elliott and Henry Edwards, who also had the Dorset Arms at nearby Hartfield, and was run by John Spencer. It still retains its huge open fireplace in front of which a vestry meeting was held in 1820 to which poor parents of children of 11 years of age or more were summoned 'to order the putting out of such children to service'.

WIVELSFIELD

ROYAL OAK: On the night of 26th May 1734, this coaching inn on the Haywards Heath to Brighton Road was the scene of a multiple murder. A Jewish pedlar called Jacob Harris slit the landlord's throat with a razor, then murdered his wife and a serving wench.

Harris was a regular visitor to the inn so when he turned up on that night in May the landlord, Richard Miles, helped him unsaddle his horse. Suddenly Harris attacked him with a razor and, leaving him for dead, went indoors, murdered the two women and left with what valuables he could lay his hands on. When he returned to the stables to get his horse he found that the landlord whom he had left for dead had disappeared. Badly hurt as he was Richard Miles had managed to crawl away to get assistance and he did not die before he had been able to identify his assailant.

Harris rode away with all speed but was apprehended two days later at an inn near Turners Hill. He was tried for murder, convicted and hanged at Horsham. His body was cut down from the gibbet and brought to Ditchling Common where it was hung in chains from what is still known as Jacob's Post, a fragment of which survives suspended from the ceiling of the bar at the Royal Oak.

Richard Miles was buried in Wivelsfield churchyard with his wife, Dorothy. The maid, Dorrity, was also buried there.

Shelley's Hotel, Lewes

Appendix I

INN SIGNS

A bunch of ivy or vine leaves hanging outside was the Roman way of saying that inside there was wine for sale. They introduced this form of advertising when they conquered Britain and when they left the practice was continued. Not always were there vine leaves or ivy to hand so the alewives would attach any sort of evergreenery to the end of a pole and put it outside when they had wine for sale. The pole, or alestake, was considered sufficient if they just had a new brew of ale. Two are shown in the Bayeux Tapestry – on the house next to one that has been set on fire.

After 1267, when the Assize of Bread and Ale regulated the price and quality of a brew, the alestake was also a method of summoning the ale-conner or ale-taster. This local official's job was to test the ale before it was sold and categorise it as small or strong ale. This he did by smell, sight and taste and not, unless he was exceptionally eccentric, by pouring some ale on a wooden bench and sitting on it for half an hour to see if it would stick his leather breeches to the planking. Versions of this apocryphal story vary – some saying that if the breeches stick the ale is of top quality, others saying the reverse is the case.

As ale houses increased in number their owners looked around for ways to distinguish one from another – there not being a lot one can do to make an alestake look different. They started to add carved symbols to their stakes – of such familiar things as the sun, moon, stars or perhaps a bull's head or a plough share. This early form of folk art was encouraged by Richard II who ruled in 1393 that anyone brewing ale for sale would forfeit it if a sign was not displayed.

By the 17th century the signs had become wonders as innkeepers vied with each other in al fresco advertising. Largest of the lot was the extravaganza outside the White Hart

119

at Scole in Norfolk which in 1655 cost more than £1,000 to make. It arched across the road and was supported by pillars covered with carvings of mythological creatures. From the centre of the arch hung an almost life size white hart surrounded by a frieze of carved wood. Signs of this sort were a hazard to the carriages which passed beneath them and they were banned by an Act of Parliament in 1797.

The George at Rye had such a sign when it was in the Butchery. It was so extravagant in size and ornamentation that it quite overshadowed the town hall and the Corporation of Rye complained bitterly about it. The inn was transferred to a Tudor house in the High Street in 1719 and the gallows type sign was moved too, but once again the Corporation complained and it had to be taken down.

More orthodox inn signs – painted boards hanging from cast or wrought iron brackets – have changed little in the past 500 years. They divide naturally into categories. There are signs of religious significance such as the Lambs, the Three Kings, the Mitre; the heraldic signs such as the White Hart, badge of Richard II, the Red Lion of John of Gaunt; signs associated with sports such as the Cricketers, Fox and Hounds, Bat and Ball; signs indicating local occupations such as the Limeburners, Bricklayers, Sawyers, and Potters Arms; and those associated with the sea – the Ships, Anchors, Smugglers.

The most popular of all signs, in the county and in the country, is the Crown. Other reflections of royalty are the Kings Heads, Kings Arms, Queens Heads and, of course, the many Royal Oaks. Charles II's flight path through Sussex after his defeat at the Battle of Worcester in 1651 is marked by inns of this name – few of which he visited and many of which he did not even pass. But John Pendrell had a good reason for changing the name of the White Horse in Lewes to the Royal Oak in 1814 when he took it over. His grandfather, then a doctor at Alfriston, was a lineal descendant of the Pendrell brothers who had hidden the king after Worcester and he was in receipt of a State pension granted by Charles after the Restoration.

And then there are the odd signs – the ones intended to make people smile. East Sussex has two good examples of these punning signs. At Warbleton there is the Warbill-in-Tun with a sign showing an axe or warbill embedded in a barrel or tun. And at Heathfield there is the Runt-in-Tun, the sign of which depicts a little pink pig in a barrel. The reason for this strange name? The pub is in the hamlet of Runtington.

Inn signs often cause local arguments. 'Why' ask knowledgeable locals 'does the recently painted sign outside the Roebuck at Forest Row show a red deer stag instead of a roebuck?' The artist's reply is awaited.

Another puzzle is why the inn at Jevington is called the Eight Bells when the parish church of St Andrew, just down the lane, has only two bells – and it never has had any more.

Playing 'cricket' with inn signs is something that even adults in cars have been known to do – to entertain the children, of course. One side bowls, the other bats. Batsmen score runs by making a quick count of the legs (if any) shown on the sign. The Fox scores four; the Hare and Hounds as many as there are hounds, multiplied by four, and do not forget the hare. The bowling side gets a wicket every time a sign is spotted without legs or 'runs' – for instance, the Star, Half Moon, Royal Oak and so on.

The Cricketers Arms, Berwick

Appendix II

INN GAMES

Darts and dominoes, quoits and cribbage, shove ha'penny and snooker, bowls and billiards – nowadays petanque and pool – all are games played in pubs or outside them.

In the past the sports were crueller. The average pub patron of the 17th to 19th centuries saw nothing odd or cruel in cock fighting, bear and badger baiting, even clergymen indulged in throwing at cocks at Eastertide. As many people spent their working lives in hunting, shooting or fishing to feed their families, the death of a bird or an animal meant nothing to them if it was done in the way of sport.

It was not until the 19th century that legislation banned the bull and badger baits and the cock fights that had been so popular with the patrons of the inns of Sussex. A few cockpits remain – there is one at Goodwood – and some bulls got away with it, as at Hove in 1810 when the baited animal broke its rope and charged the crowd.

Indoor games, however, have had a much harder time. Various governments have legislated against games of chance and often the issue of a licence for an alehouse depended on conditions forbidding the playing of dice, dominoes, assorted card games and skittles 'at the time of divine service'. The Puritans were particularly punitive. Not only did they legislate against the playing of games. They forbad maypole dancing and horse racing as well.

The traditional pub games of Sussex have survived in spite of everything. There are plenty of places where they still play ring the bull, devil among the tailors, toad-in-the-hole. At Hastings they even play loggetts, a game banned in the 17th century.

Darts is, of course, the most popular of all pub games. It became a national craze between the wars and now there are some 6 to 7 million regular players. It may have originated as a knife throwing or indoor archery contest using the end of a beer cask as the target.

Dominoes probably originated in China but was introduced to England by the French prisoners of war in the 18th century. It was because he lost at a version of the game called All Fours that Robert Clarke, the Horsham public executioner, hanged himself in the hayloft of the Anchor Inn in 1749. What really worried him was that the money he lost had been entrusted to him to buy a pig.

Shove ha'penny, or shove penny as it is often called in Sussex because the metal discs are larger, dates from Tudor times. It is played on a wooden board divided into sections with strips of brass. The object is to get a total of three discs into each 'bed' or strip.

Snooker, billiards and bar billiards, as well as the later arrival, pool, can be found in town pubs which have the space for a separate games room. These games also turn up in the resort towns and holiday villages where often the pub is also the local entertainment centre like the Ship at Winchelsea Beach.

Marbles, of course, means the Greyhound at Tinsley Green, where the British Individual Marbles Championships are held every Good Friday. But the game is also played at Battle on Good Friday – before 12 noon of course. Anyone playing marbles after that time would have them confiscated and stamped into the ground.

Two games or pastimes that crop up in occasional pubs in East and West Sussex are toad-in-the-hole and ringing the bull.

Toad-in-the-hole requires the competitors to throw heavy metal discs into a hole in the centre of a lead cushion mounted on a low table with a drawer in it. Competitors stand 8 feet away from the target and score two points for every disc that goes into the hole, one point for each one that remains on the cushion, and nothing for the ones that fall to the ground. The object is to score 31 points and this score must be achieved exactly – you bust if you score 32 and must try again for the exact number.

Ringing the bull has its variations throughout Sussex. In

some pubs, such as the Blackboys Inn at Blackboys, the 'bull' is a stag's head, in others it can be just a hook on the wall or a complete bull's head or perhaps just the horns. A metal ring hangs from a line attached to the ceiling and the object of the exercise is to swing it across the room so it lands on the target. In the Swan at Lewes in the 1930s there was a regular customer who would stand with his back to the bull and ring the hook in its nose every time.

Devil among the Tailors is a form of table skittles which originated in the 18th century, It is not often met with today. Real skittles, the outdoor sort, are played at the Black Horse in Findon, and at the Wilkes Head at Eastergate they have introduced the game so popular with the French, boule.

Funny fund raising games such as dwile flonking (allegedly invented by the students of Leeds University in a rag week in the 1960s), wellie throwing, piano bashing, china breaking, have their place in the social scene but cannot be taken too seriously. Video and quiz games also come and go ..... but darts go on for ever.

Bibliography

Shergold's Recollections of Brighton in Olden Times.
Brighton and its Coaches, W.C.A. Blew, 1893.
Life in Brighton, Clifford Musgrave, John Halliwell
   Publications, 1981.
The Old Ship – A Prospect of Brighton, Raymond Flower 1986.
Eastbourne Memories, George F. Chambers.
Historic Hastings, J. Manwaring Baines, F.J. Parson 1953.
Hailsham and its Environs, Charles A. Robertson, 1980.
History of Hove, H.C. Porter.
History of Hove, Judy Middleton, Phillimore 1979.
Guide to Rye, William Holloway, 1888.
Tudor Rye, Graham Mayhew, University of Sussex 1987.
History of Salehurst, L.J. Hodson.
History of Seaford. Seaford Museum of Local History.
Uckfield Visitors' Guide, 1869.
Udimore Past and Present, L.J. Hodson, 1905.
Our Sussex Parish. Thomas Geering 1925.
Coast of Sussex. J.D. Parry, 1833.
Old English Mills and Inns, R. Thurston Hopkins, 1927.
Inns of Sport, Whitbread and Co. 1949.
CAMRA Real Ale and *Real Pubs in Sussex*, 1987.
The English – A Social History 1066–1945, Christopher Hibbert,
   Grafton Books 1987.
Bexhill Observer.
Hastings Observer.
Eastbourne Chronicle.
Sussex Daily News
Sussex Express and County Herald.
Sussex Weekly Advertiser
Kelly's Directories. 1874–1938.
East Sussex Records Office, The Maltings, Lewes.
Sussex Archeological Collections.

Sussex County Magazine
Sussex Notes and Queries.
The Gentleman's Magazine.
Sussex Life.